Building & Maintaining
Docks

How to Design, Build, Install & Care for Residential Docks

Chris Lamping

**Creative Publishing
international**

CHANHASSEN, MINNESOTA
www.creativepub.com

Creative Publishing
international

Copyright © 2007
Creative Publishing international, Inc.
18705 Lake Drive East
Chanhassen, Minnesota 55317
1-800-328-3895
www.creativepub.com
All rights reserved

Printed in China

10 9 8 7 6 5 4 3 2 1

President/CEO: Ken Fund

Publisher: Bryan Trandem

Author: Chris Lamping
Editor: Mark Johanson
Art Director: Jon Simpson
Assistant Managing Editor: Tracy Stanley
Photo Acquisitions Editor: Julie Caruso
Production Manager: Linda Halls, Laura Hokkanen

CONTENTS

Library of Congress Cataloging-in-Publication Data

Lamping, Chris,
  Building & maintaining docks : how to design, build, install & care for residential docks / Chris Lamping.
    p. cm.
  Summary: "A guide book for planning, designing, building, and maintaining any type of dock, both for primary residences and vacation homes"--Provided by publisher.
  ISBN-13: 978-1-58923-284-6 (soft cover)
  ISBN-10: 1-58923-284-4 (soft cover)
  1. Docks--Design and construction. I. Title. II. Title: Building and maintaining docks.

TC355.L36 2007
627'.31--dc22

2006028094

INTRODUCTION

WITHOUT A DOCK, WATERFRONT PROPERTY CAN NEVER BE USED AND ENJOYED TO ITS FULLEST POTENTIAL. SWIMMING, FISHING, ENTERTAINING, OR JUST SITTING IN QUIET CONTEMPLATION ALL ARE MADE EASIER AND SAFER BY THE PRESENCE OF A GOOD, STURDY DOCK.

Even if your first reaction to the suggestion that you build a dock yourself is "Who, me?", give the idea some consideration. After all, dock building may be a somewhat unusual do-it-yourself pursuit, but there is nothing unusually difficult about it. And for those of us whose watery getaway is in a remote area, the DIY approach may be the only option.

Any skepticism you encounter when announcing your dock-building plan may have its roots in the fact that, unless it's wobbling wildly or drifting away from shore attached to your bass boat, a dock can be one of those mundane conveniences that we just don't think much about. But as with any structure (or vehicle or pet or mysterious rash, for that matter) the best time to think about docks is before you have a problem. By taking the time to learn more about docks and how they are made and maintained, you can design and build your dream dock on your own terms and schedule.

A dock can be a highly romantic structure, conjuring pleasant images of placid water or sunsplashed fun with the family. But building docks is serious business and the consequences of making mistakes can be very high. In our examination of docks and dock building, let's leave fond remembrances of quirky character and creaking gangways behind and instead focus on building something that will provide solid footing for fun times.

PORTFOLIO OF DOCKS

A DOCK THAT'S CAREFULLY CONCEIVED, WELL PLANNED, AND SOLIDLY CONSTRUCTED HAS GREAT VALUE HOWEVER IT'S USED: AS A HUB OF SOCIAL AND RECREATIONAL ACTIVITY FOR YOUR WATERFRONT PROPERTY; TO MOOR BOATS AND OTHER WATERCRAFT; TO PROVIDE A STABLE JUMPING-OFF POINT FOR SWIMMING; TO CREATE A SAFE SPOT TO FISH; OR SIMPLY AS A QUIET PLACE TO SIT AND WATCH THE SUNSET ON THE WATER. IT SHOULD DO ALL OF THESE THINGS IN SUCH A WAY THAT ALL YOU HAVE TO THINK ABOUT IS THE ACTIVITY AT HAND.

If you've ever attempted to play football or baseball on a field that's littered with trash or jutting rocks and stumps or pitted with holes, you've had the experience of thinking more about avoiding the emergency room than enjoying the game. A dock is no different—while you might wax nostalgic about your uncle's creaky, unpredictable floating dock that you used as a child, the fact is that you probably would have caught more fish if that dock wasn't announcing your presence to your quarry.

Because so much of the dock-design process involves matching form to function, begin by reviewing the photographs on the following pages. You'll see some fairly consistent patterns in the way the layouts are created. And also watch for any accessories or decorative features that you find appealing. Docks can be extremely simple in design, but that doesn't mean they can't be unique creations.

The Classic American dock is designed to accommodate all of the most popular water activities, but in an efficient package that's easy to put in and take out of the water. The L configuration of the principal structure provides a clear walkway and even seating areas. The angled finger section establishes a mini-marina for the boat and personal watercraft, and the floating swim raft can be anchored in just the right spot.

Fabricated dock systems with a rigid aluminum undercarriage are installed in sections that are usually joined together in the water. Decking is often panelized and removable.

A well-designed dock functions as a continuation of the shoreline area, especially when it abuts built environments like the large paver patio above.

If you've ever vacationed at a freshwater lake in North America, you've seen this dock. You wouldn't want to host an entire rugby team on it, but for weekend family use it does what you need it to do.

A long, narrow dock has a certain elegance, especially when it extends out from a defined point of land. The length also allows access to multiple areas of the lake. Here, a dock ladder rises up out of the water in a sandy swimming area, while at the end of the dock a swiveling bench is poised perfectly over a prime fishing hole.

Some docks function very much like bridges, linking the comforts of land with the open expanses of water. You can look at the picture from shore, then cross the bridge and become part of it.

A well-equipped dock structure creates new living space where once there was only water. With the addition of a swiveling deck chair at a sunny corner, this deck becomes more than simply a way to board your boat without getting your feet wet: it becomes a destination to be shared.

The clean, cool water a few feet out from the shoreline often is perfect for swimming. With the addition of a simple L dock, swimmers can access the water without the hazards of walking over slippery rocks in the shallows.

Storing and mooring watercraft is but one of the benefits a sturdy dock offers. With your canoe or kayak ready and waiting on the dock, you can slip off into the glass-calm water at the very moment the sunset is perfect.

Low maintenance is an important dock-design detail for many waterfront property owners. What's the point of getting away for the weekend if you spend the entire time cleaning? For many, the perfect dock is the smallest possible size to accomplish a single primary purpose, such as mooring a speedboat. And if it's easy to take in and out of the water, all the better.

Aluminum, plastic, and pressure treated-decking all have their advantages, but for striking beauty it's hard to beat natural cedar. If you are building your dock from lumber with rich wood tones, be aware that you'll need to strip it and recoat it with UV protectant at least once or twice a year to keep the wood from graying.

You can choose to build a huge, sprawling dock that looms over the waterfront and impresses all the boatersby with its opulence and beauty. But in the end, the best docks are the ones that bring the water safely into the lives of your family and friends. If your new dock puts a smile on a young face, you may truly call it a success.

DOCK BASICS

WHERE THE FIRST FUNCTION OF A DOCK IS A KIND OF QUIET UTILITY, A DOCK SHOULD BE THOUGHT OF AS AN EXTENSION OF YOUR LAND INTO THE WATER.

A dock is a kind of bridge between neighbors that begins on one waterfront dweller's private land and extends into a common area seen and used by everyone on the waterfront. While good fences may make good neighbors to the landlocked, good docks make good neighbors on the waterfront. Unlike your landlocked home, which you can fence in or wall in as you please, your waterfront home is always, to some degree anyway, open and exposed for public scrutiny. In fact, you could say that the view of your lake property almost belongs more to your neighbors than it does to you. With this in mind, remember the golden rule: "Do unto others as you would have them do unto you." Chances are that if you set the example of building a structure that is pleasant to look at and well integrated with both your property and the water, your neighbors will follow suit.

> *"While good fences may make good neighbors to the landlocked, good docks make good neighbors on the waterfront."*

As you consider your new dock, keep in mind that it will not function only as a bridge between land and water; it will become part of the environment. There are animals and plantlife that share the land and water with you and your family, whose habits and activities will be shaped by the structure you build. Keep this in mind as you prepare to build. Just as you are affecting the aesthetics of the waterfront when you build a structure on it, you are affecting the ecosystem of the lake or stream when you build something into it. If you wrap a sapling in barbed wire, the tree will be forced to grow around it as it matures, in short, it will grow *differently* than if you had never been there. Affecting the ecosystem is not necessarily a bad thing: it can be, but doesn't have to be. A carelessly placed dock could wipe out a spawning ground for fish, just as a well-thought-out structure could provide those same fish with shelter from airborne predators. It might also provide a nice vantage point for those tasty fish to see the interesting-looking shiny objects that periodically drop into the water!

Take the time to learn about the environment you are building on, and remember that it is almost impossible to build a fully neutral structure with relation to the environment. You must ask yourself what sort of impact you want to have on the local environment. The more you are able to learn about that environment, the more likely it will be that the impact you desire to make with your structure will match the impact you actually have.

PLANNING YOUR NEW DOCK

The first step in building a dock is to figure out what it is you have *before* you start. This step is not to be taken lightly, and a careful, thorough assessment of what you will be building on will help you assess all of the concerns described above.

First, start collecting. Those snapshots you've taken throughout the years don't merely capture the first Northern Pike your son caught when he was eight—they undoubtedly also capture vital dock-building information about the land, water, seasons, and uses.

Family photos taken on and around your waterfront property may provide clues to where you should site your new dock and how you should configure it.

Consider exactly where water activities take place when siting your dock. If your waterfront includes a shoaly area that's hazardous for boating, for example, design your dock so the mooring sections are far away from the danger zone. If you have a favorite swimming spot, locate the dock near, but not in, that spot.

Look more closely. What's behind him? What do you remember about that moment? Who is behind him, and what were they doing? Where did he catch the fish? Have others also caught fish from that spot? Are certain activities and uses one-time activities or uses, or are there other times that people have done these things? Often? Or once in a while? What times of year are people doing these things? Obviously (unless you're the hockey team that drowned during spring training), you don't try to skate year-round on the lake, but is there a spot that seems like it gets used for that purpose more often

than another when you do? What about swimming? Fishing? These are the kinds of things you'll need to begin thinking about.

While you will first want to assess the land, flora, and fauna, remember that some of the fauna are bipeds: that is, you, your family, and friends. If you have a place that is particularly good for swimming, do you really want to build a dock in that place with the notion that people will just start swimming off the dock instead? If something is particularly good for a certain purpose, then perhaps you won't want

If you use your waterfront property year-round, take seasonal factors into account. For example, avoid siting your dock in spots that will disrupt a favorite wintertime naturescape.

to disrupt that purpose. Remember: you *know* you like swimming from that place; you might like swimming off the dock better, or you may hate it. Do you want to take that chance? If possible, why *not* have your cake and eat it too? If you have a fantastic swimming hole, then is swimming what you really need to build a dock for as well?

So, as you take these strolls down memory lane, you should start to recognize patterns, activities, things, and places that repeat. While some will tell you that your first act should be to think about the land with no people on it, if you begin by discarding information only to try to add it in later, you'll have a potential mess on your hands. For starters, you are attempting to compile as much information as you possibly can about the land, ecosystem, and its uses. Get yourself some file folders and as things occur to you in looking back over your snapshots, start writing categories on those folders: Fishing, Swimming, Wildlife, Picnics, Games, whatever occurs to you as you go along. Start with bigger categories: you can always make things more specific later.

Consult with your family and friends. If, for example, you're off golfing every day in warm weather and your spouse and children are at the cabin together all day, it is quite possible that there is a whole range of activities about which you know next to nothing.

The point is to begin to put together a "big picture," identify patterns (not just your own) and discard anomalies—if your daughter caught a sunfish in one spot, one time, then later, as you site your dock, you probably won't want to preserve that spot as a fishing hole. If, however, your fisherman neighbor finds that to be a particularly good spot to fish for walleye at 4:30 A.M., when you're asleep, you might want to take that into account.

Soon, you'll start to round the picture out nicely, and will be ready to start mapping the area. For this, it is best to get yourself some graph paper. You'll want to use graph paper because this will allow you to maintain a sense of proportion and relationship. The scale of your drawing will depend on the size of your property. Ideally, you'll be able to locate survey markers that will give you the broad canvas with which to work, but if those are no longer in evidence, you'll need to get a map from your local registrar of deeds, and if you are still unable to find the survey markers, you may have to contract a professional surveyor.

For now, you're only interested in the land itself. In addition to family snapshots, you'll want to take photographs of your shoreline and attached land, and where possible, in as many different times of the year as you are able. Ideally, you will have a good sense of the view of the waterfront in all four seasons, and your final design will be smart year-round.

Once you've mapped the visible topography of your land, you'll need to start thinking about things not captured in photographs. If tides are an issue, measure

both the advance and retreat of the water level and mark them on your map. Do you draw water from the lake or stream? If so, you'll need to include the water-intake line. Are ice-flows an issue on your waterfront? If so, you'll need to take into account the water-level rise brought about by ice jams. What is the maximum shade line on your waterfront? Draw it in. Does your waterfront flood? If so, how much and how regularly? If there was a huge flood back in the spring of '43, but things have been tame since, you likely don't need to fret too much about such possibilities. If, on the other hand, your stream regularly floods, then you'll need to mark the maximum advance of the water line on your map in relation to the mean.

Which way do the prevailing winds go? Make a notation. Are there substantial currents on your waterfront? You'll need to note these as well.

Acquire any maps you can to help you plot out your dock plan. Your state department of natural resources may be able to provide a survey map of your lake, for example. Use the maps as a starting point for drawing a map of your property.

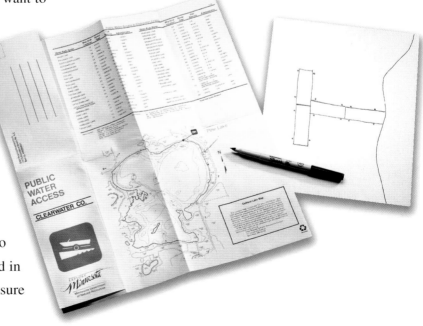

Now, what about nature? While underwater grasses may be icky to swim in and tanglers of fishing lines, remember that these are breeding and feeding grounds for aquatic life. More than that, these plants perform the valuable function of converting carbon dioxide in the lake into water-suspended oxygen that fish and water-born critters require to live. If you were to drop a giant crib dock into that patch of weeds that you don't consider good for anything anyway, you could be wiping out your chances of catching fish by getting rid of that little inconvenience as well.

Finally, you'll need to get wet. Because a significant portion of what the dock will be used for (not to mention what it's built on or anchored in) will be underwater, you'll need to take measurements of what you're dealing with beneath the surface.

A new dock impacts the environment it is in, both positively and negatively. The shade a dock casts can stress aquatic plant life, but it can also provide shelter for fish when predators are about.

Does your shoreline drop off? If so, how far out into the water? You'll need to note the distance between the normal water advance and the drop-off point about every 10 to 15 feet along the shoreline. If it doesn't drop off precipitously (clifflike), you'll need to measure the water level going out from shore. By taking these measurements, you'll be getting a sense of what you will be dealing with beneath the water, and you'll be able to create a map of your underwater topography. If you are a fisherman and own an electronic fish locator, you may be able to use that piece of equipment to take some useful readings of your lakeshore or riverbed.

Finally, wade and swim around. You will in all likelihood have discovered any potential underwater impediments to boating or dock construction, but it never hurts to do a bit of snorkeling to see what else is down there.

ACTIVITIES AND PEOPLE

Now that you have a map of your shoreline, and an underwater topography, it's time to start putting those folders mentioned above to use. In order to complete planning for your dock, you'll need to think about what you intend to build it for, and for whom.

The latter is the easiest, and you should be able to make a list in a very short time. Who is going to use this dock? Start by listing your family members and their respective ages. Now, who else do you anticipate using the dock? Do you have friends or neighbors who regularly visit your cabin and would also use the dock? List them as well. Are you expecting to have children (or more of them)? What about grandchildren? As you plan for the dock, you'll want to take likely changes in the size

Measure water depth at multiple times over the year. Use the low-water mark when designing and siting your dock (shallow water creates problems for docks and watercraft).

Use a story pole (any straight wood stick) to measure the water depth in many locations around the potential dock area. Have a helper record and map the measurements as you yell them out.

of your group into account. What about pets? A Chihuahua probably won't have much of an impact on space and usage considerations, but much bigger than that, you're going to want to make allowances for your furry friend(s).

Finally, are there any special needs? If, for example, you've got a friend or family member who relies on a wheelchair, you want to be sure to build a dock with easy accessibility.

Also, list the number and sizes of watercraft that will be moored at your dock. If you already have a suitable canoe launch, you probably won't include

that, but if you have a steep, clifflike shoreline, then chances are you'll want to launch your canoe from the dock instead of negotiating the incline. Consider also that as the size of your family increases, so will your needs for a larger craft to moor at your dock. Alternately, you might simply be planning on buying a bigger boat down the line someday, and so should plan for that.

The point of these exercises is to determine both what you have and what you want. Having reached these conclusions, the design and planning process begins to get more concrete.

Keep the shape and configuration of your dock as simple as you possibly can. For sheer versatility, a basic rectangle outpaces all other shapes. Using rectangles, you can devise an overall configuration that meets your exact needs for size and functionality.

DOCK CONFIGURATIONS

IT MIGHT MAKE AN INTERESTING REMARK TO SUGGEST THAT DOCKS COME IN ALL SHAPES AND SIZES, BUT IT WOULDN'T BE PARTICULARLY ACCURATE. THEY MAY COME IN ALL SIZES, BUT AS A GENERAL RULE YOU'LL FIND THAT DOCKS TEND TO BE VARIATIONS ON ONE SHAPE: THE RECTANGLE.

There are exceptions, some of which are quite stunning, and we'll look at those below. But you'll find that even the exceptions are ultimately variations on the old parallelogram.

Why is this so? Well, the first reason is stability. It's just easier to negotiate a structure on which the corners are identical. The second reason is simple utility. It might look cool if your dock has a bat-cave-inspired custom slip that fits your cigarette boat like a glove, but you won't be able to park a regular boat there, and the dock probably won't be good for much else, either. Just remember, the more specifically your dock is built for a particular purpose, the less likely it is that it will be suitable for other tasks.

Overall size is important to dock stability, although the type of support system the dock employs is related to stability and size, as you'll see in later chapters. A larger dock is usually more stable; you can do more things on it, and accommodate more people with it.

A larger dock is also able to withstand inclement weather and wave conditions and moor larger boats due to the simple fact that all of these things pulling and pushing it every which way have a lot more to pull and push with a larger structure. Think of a sled. It's a lot more difficult to get a sled going when it's fully loaded—usually someone has to get off and push. But once a heavily loaded sled gets going, look out! There isn't too much that's going to stop it, and the same is true of a dock. Your boat certainly is no match for such a massive structure overtaking it.

The benefits a large dock offers when it comes to stability, increased deck space, and overall versatility may be offset by the environmental impact or the cost. Also on the downside, big docks can mean backaches and headaches when the time comes to remove them for winter or put them back in the water in the spring. Most states or local governments limit the allowable size of a dock installed for a private residence. For example, in

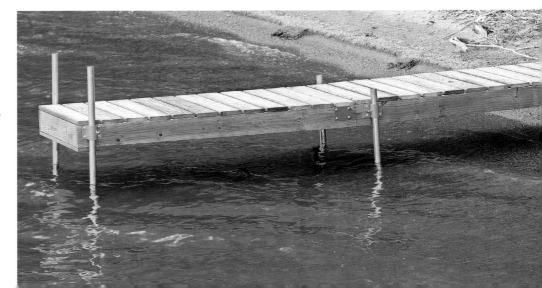

Most dock configurations are created by joining a series of modular sections. For maximum efficiency, build all of the sections to the same size and shape.

A long, straight dock can be used for practically any water activity, including fishing, boating, and even suntanning and swimming.

Minnesota any dock wider than 8 ft. requires a commercial permit. You also can't make the dock as long as you please, for obvious reasons of navigation. So as much as you'd love to build a 120-ft. dock out to your favorite sandbar, what you'd actually be building is something entirely different, commonly known as a bridge.

Small docks typically are less expensive to build than their bigger cousins, although one advantage to building small is that you may be able to afford higher-grade building materials because you'll need less. Small docks also have a proportionally smaller impact on the environment and are much lighter, making for easier removal in winter. At the same time, a smaller dock can be disastrous if you hitch a very large boat to it, or if you site it in a spot that will take a serious pounding from weather and waves. And the smaller the dock is, the fewer things you will be able to do with it.

SHAPE

The rectangle, pretty much out of necessity, will find itself incorporated into just about every dock configuration. Very simply, the rectangle is what gets you out onto the water and creates a nicely symmetrical structure from which all manner and shape of add-ons can be launched. Boards are rectangles, and if you put two rectangles together in just such a way, you create a larger rectangle.

But the basic rectangle design should not be discounted as too ho-hum. A simple rectangle gets you out into the water, and if it isn't particularly rough water, you can tie up a boat to one side and still have room on the other side for other activities. In some circumstances, a simple rectangle might be all that the property lines will allow. If you've got a narrow shoreline, your neighbors likely won't much appreciate your annexation of their waterfront, and a rectangle might then be the only structure you can build there. Moreover, the simple rectangle will be easier on the budget, and easier to remove and replace. The simplicity of the rectangle makes it very flexible from a design standpoint.

The limitations to the basic rectangular shape are easy enough to discern. It won't allow for too many activities at the same time. Families trying to fish, swim, sunbathe, and dock a boat all at once will likely end up with someone getting wet, and

not necessarily the ones intent on a swim. In other words, the basic rectangle can get pretty crowded pretty quickly.

Adding more rectangles to your basic rectangle is the fundamental activity of designing a dock. Choosing where to put the new rectangles and how many to build is driven largely by the activities you want your deck to support. The most common types of additions to a basic rectangle create L and T shapes, so called because they form those shapes.

The advantage of the T shape is that it provides a bit of safe harbor to each side of the dock in certain circumstances, also making it possible for multiple uses of the dock space at the same time. Thus, you can fish to one side while the kids swim to the other. Adding a T also increases the stability of your

T-shape docks provide useful safe harbor on two sides, making them a good choice if you'll be tying up a couple of watercraft at the same time.

L-shape docks provide a larger harbor area and are popular choices when paired with a ramped boat hoist on the open leg.

structure—whether you are building a floating dock or a pipe dock, figure that the T acts something like training wheels or flying buttresses on a cathedral. Side-to-side movement is simply more difficult if there is side support. The T allows you to moor several small boats to either side in the limited safe harbor created by the structure, and if waves are not a significant issue, a larger boat along the long end.

The L shape also provides increased space and functionality to your dock design, but in different ways. While the T shape gave a limited safe harbor to each side, the L takes from one column and adds it to the other. So, on one side, you essentially have the long unbroken surface of the simple rectangle, and on the other, an extended safe harbor for mooring a larger craft. Families that utilize a water railway can moor their boat to one side, and place the railway to the long end of the dock. The L provides increased stability (though not so much as the T), and increased functionality, though again not so much as the T.

In addition to increased stability, both the L and T shapes offer potential seating areas for entertainment that are not shared with the access area. Thus, you can set up lawn chairs or even build a bench into your deck, and not have the same issues of everyone having to stand up and move out of the way constantly.

Other Shapes. The universe of dock configurations goes well beyond straight, T, and L. A little like one of those bar games in which you can move X number of straws to create a desired structure, the only limitation here is that your structure has to incorporate straight lines. Say your family isn't so

Platform docks provide plenty of square footage for comfortable lounging and entertaining involving larger groups of people. You create them by adding sections side to side instead of end to end.

T platform docks have the advantage of a more expansive deck area, and they project further out from shore with the addition of a gangway section.

much interested in boating, but does like to have a good number of folks over, enjoys sunbathing, swimming, and just hanging out. Instead of adding rectangular sections end-to-end or in an L or T, you can add them to the sides to create a roomier, more stable platform.

Suddenly, with a simple addition, you've created a very comfortable space for just such activities, and you still have plenty of room to moor a craft to either side. You can get your enhanced platform farther out into the water simply by adding another rectangle as a kind of gangway.

If your lake life centers around your boat, a U shape is a common dock configuration. People who own pontoon boats, in particular, enjoy this shape because it positions the boat at the middle of the party, so you can easily climb aboard and enjoy a few boat drinks without the trouble of heading out to sea.

With a little imagination, there is virtually no end to the number of configurations you can devise for a dock. And because most docks are designed to be modular, you can even change the shape from time to time if you hit upon a better idea. For example, an enclosed square configuration might seem like a great idea because you can float all day on your air mattress with your trusty floating cooler at your side without worrying about drifting over to Pastor Olson's place. But if you find out that the shape proves irresistible to your slightly manic golden retriever that enjoys nothing more than dashing around and around in circles all day, you can still go back to a more conventional shape with relative ease. Your only limitations are the amount of money you have to spend, local wildlife and plant life, and local regulations.

U docks form a cozy harbor between the uprights of the U. Popular for mooring pontoon boats, this dock configuration also brings the boat itself into the heart of the entertainment area.

Enclosed square docks are a bit unconventional, but they have the advantage of creating a confined swimming or floating area, a bit like your own personal swimming pool.

FINGER DOCKS

Finger docks are designed and built to accommodate multiple boats. Often you will see them at marinas or at multi unit waterfront housing developments.

The fingers on a finger dock can be the same width as the main dock section. But to maximize the number of slips that can be created, you can use narrower catwalk sections, as long as they are at least 24" wide. The catwalks are a bit unstable compared to full-width dock sections, but they normally provide adequate support for boarding and disembarking.

Four examples of finger docks are shown on this page, with the top two featuring narrow catwalk configurations.

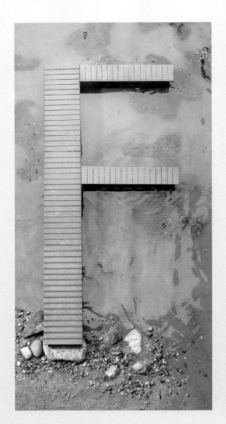

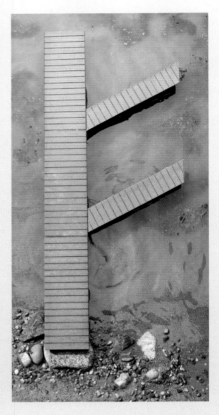

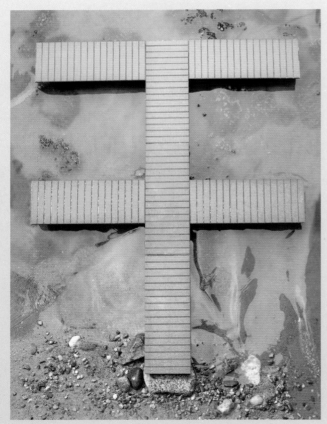

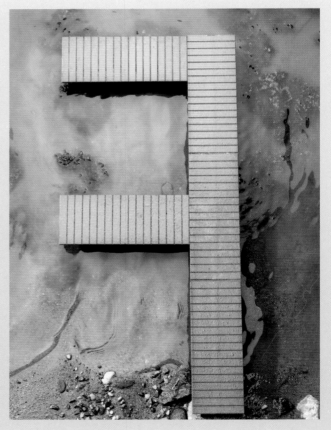

SWIMMING RAFTS

The ultimate single-purpose docks, swimming rafts are almost always supported with floats and can normally be accessed only by swimming or via small watercraft. A securely attached ladder is highly recommended.

Although the tanning dock is constructed in much the same manner as a shorefront dock, a swimming raft isn't typically thought of as being a dock. Usually constructed with floats beneath the deck to make it buoyant, a swimming raft must be securely anchored, generally in at least two points. For safety reasons, you want to be sure that the raft remains in essentially the same spot.

In addition to ample support and a large deck for reclining, a swimming raft should be equipped with a swimming ladder and a few mooring points for tying up inner tubes or small watercraft. Also attach safety reflectors on all sides of the raft frame to prevent accidents with night-time boaters.

Many types of floats may be used to support a swimming raft, including plastic tubes. Don't use old 55-gallon barrels.

DOCKS FOR FISHING

If, for you, fishing is a close family activity requiring immediate supervision, site your dock near (but not over) a fishing hotspot (you may even find that the shade afforded by the dock attracts fish). A wide dock (at least 4 ft.) is a good choice for family fishing. The last thing you want is to be cramped together when you're helping a small fishing companion bait a hook.

If you plan to do a lot of fishing from your dock (a time-honored way to while away a pleasant summer afternoon), design a dock that has multiple end points, such as a T dock, or even a cross-shaped dock like the one on the next page. This allows the dock to accommodate more than one fisherman, or perhaps a single angler who can be secluded enough to safely cast a line while others enjoy the dock in other ways. Also, the more end points your dock has, the more chances you'll have to find a spot where the fish are biting.

You'll also want to have a good spot for tying a stringer or bait bucket, and remember to secure cleats or anchor posts for tying up a fishing boat. If you're a serious angler who eats the catch of the day, look into adding a fish-cleaning stand.

RECOMMENDED 3-POINT DOCK CONFIGURATION FOR FISHING

This cross-shape dock configuration can accommodate at least three anglers at a time with minimal crossing of fishing lines.

OTHER SUITABLE CONFIGURATIONS

L Dock

T Dock

Straight Dock

DOCKS FOR SWIMMING & SUNBATHING

Access to the water is the number one item that a dock brings to a swimming party. A traditional swimming ladder (or even an untraditional one like that in the photo to the right) is fine, but for extra safety and a bit of luxury, install a submerged stairway that connects the swimming area with the dock (see Resources, page 124). A sturdy dock also helps manage all of the water toys that inevitably accumulate.

A dock is a perfect staging area for two of the most popular water activities: swimming and sunbathing. This is particularly true if you do not have a sandy beach. To support swimming, a dock should be splinter-free and in good condition. It should have a swimming ladder and be in full view of the house or cabin. If your water is too shallow for diving, be sure to post a clearly visible sign to that effect.

A platform-type dock is ideal for the sunbathing side of things if your lot and shoreline can accommodate it.

RECOMMENDED DOCK CONFIGURATION FOR SWIMMING/SUNBATHING

This platform dock configuration has a generously sized deck area so multiple swimmers and sunbathers can enjoy the water and sun in comfort.

OTHER SUITABLE CONFIGURATIONS

T Dock

Platform Dock

T Platform Dock

DOCKS FOR ENTERTAINING

Even large docks with a big common area are easiest to build and install if they are made up of modular components. If you plan to spend large amounts of time on the dock, either alone or hosting guests, pay extra attention to the decking. Look for decking that's not too slippery when wet, but is still comfortable to sit on in a swimsuit. And choose lighter colors if they're available to keep the dock from overheating in the sun.

As with backyard decks, there's no substitute for square footage when it comes to building a dock that's equipped for a little partying. If the dock or deck is cramped and hard to move around on, guests will be uncomfortable. Keeping in mind that local restrictions may not allow extrawide platform docks, if your goal is to play host on the water, think big. On shore, set up a few of the furnishings you'd like to use to entertain on your dock. Arrange the tables and chairs and lounges so you

can move comfortably around them. Then, draw a square or rectangle around the whole setup and take measurements. You may find that your dream of having the best party dock on the lake is impossible, or too much to afford. In such cases, you may be better off relegating the big parties to the shore and simply designing a dock that's wide enough for guests to pass one another comfortably as they move between the shore and the water.

RECOMMENDED PLATFORM DOCK CONFIGURATION FOR ENTERTAINING

This modified-T platform shape creates a nicely sized entertaining area, while still allowing movement from the shore to the farthest point of the dock.

OTHER SUITABLE CONFIGURATIONS

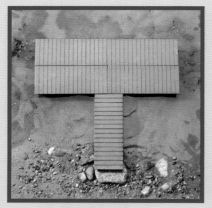

T Platform Dock

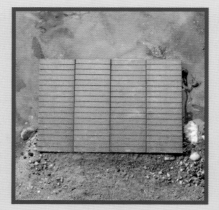

Platform Dock

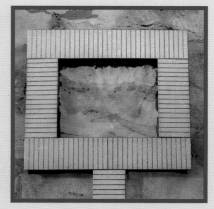

Enclosed Square Dock

DOCKS FOR BOATING

A place to park the boat, at least temporarily, and a sturdy point for stepping from the dock and onto the boat are the keys for a successful boating dock. Once you've met these basic challenges, look for ways to improve your dock by adding a covered lift and storage. Also think about adding lights so you can find the dock at night and batten everything down after a full day on the water.

Trying to design one dock for boating is like trying to find a pair of pants that everyone in the family can wear. Naturally, the most important consideration for building a boating-oriented dock is your boat (or boats). Make the dock big enough to fit it, preferably in a slip or protected area. The dock also must be well anchored so nothing drifts away when the currents are strong. A dock box and other types of seaside storage will be well appreciated when you're in the act of casting off.

RECOMMENDED DOCK CONFIGURATION FOR BOATING

The U-shape dock creates a protected sanctuary for a boat, and is often combined with a covered boat lift between the legs of the U so your watercraft may be parked right where it's needed for the entire boating season.

OTHER SUITABLE CONFIGURATIONS

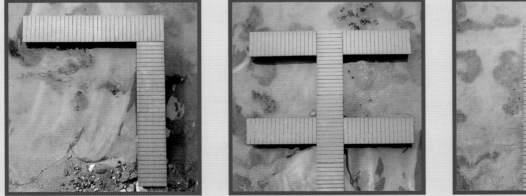
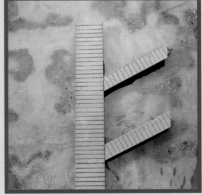

L Dock   *Finger Dock*   *Catwalk Slip Dock*

DOCK TYPES & SITING

ONCE YOU'VE BEEN THROUGH THE PROCESS OF CONSULTING WITH FAMILY AND FRIENDS, AND HAVE FIGURED OUT WHAT YOU PLAN TO USE YOUR DOCK FOR, IT'S TIME TO GET DOWN TO PLANNING THE DOCK YOU WILL ACTUALLY BUILD.

The first question to consider when selecting a dock type is whether you want a permanent dock or a removable dock. In climates where lakes and rivers freeze, a dock that can be pulled out of the water for the winter is the norm. Pipe docks, floating docks, and aluminum roll-in or tip-in docks are the most common removable dock types. Docks that are meant to be left in the water year-round generally are supported with pilings that are driven down into the lake, river, or ocean bed. Cribs are an alternative support method to pilings for permanent docks, but they are being used with decreasing frequency. So which dock is best for you? Let's consider a series of possible scenarios, keeping in mind that chances are, none of the following will exactly match your particular waterfront. But who knows, maybe you'll get lucky!

Aluminum roll-in docks are quick and easy to install and remove, making them a good choice for flat, smooth property.

THE FLOATING DOCK

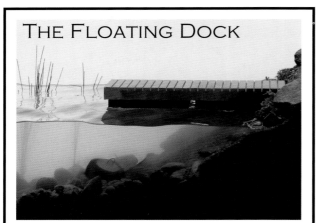

Heavy-duty plastic floats are attached to the underside of the dock deck.

Perhaps the most common and versatile of all dock types, the floating dock gets its name because it literally floats on the water aboard buoyant, hard-shell floats. Framing and decking are built on top of the floats and include a means for anchoring the dock to keep it in place. The stability of the dock is created by the positioning of the floats at the farthest outside of the structure. The entire structure is then secured with shore-based and underwater anchorage. Unlike every other dock type, the limitation on building a floating dock is shallow water of less than 3 ft. Also, a floating dock maintains the same freeboard (the distance between the deck and the water) in all water levels. So, with a floating dock, your dock won't oscillate between being a ford at one time of the year and a high-dive at another.

Floating docks, however, may not work with your site. The bare minimum for the width of a floating dock is *four feet,* and if your shoreline is narrow, this may exclude this type of dock. Moreover, because floating docks require a ratio of 1-to-3 width to length to maintain stability, the width can get well out of hand very quickly, blotting out the sun to a substantial swath of underwater vegetation.

THE PIPE DOCK

Galvanized metal pipes are attached to pipe sleeves on the dock sides to support it.

Pipe docks (sometimes called pole docks) provide perhaps the most versatile and inexpensive solution for the do-it-yourselfer. The decking and framing for a pipe dock is supported by a series of metal pipe legs that rest on the floor of a body of water. The pipe dock is usually intended to be removable.

While pipe docks are adjustable with regard to height, expect a greater fluctuation in freeboard (the distance between the dock deck and the surface of the water) with this type of dock. Pipe docks, though the least expensive to build, the easiest to modify and add onto, tend not to work well for mooring larger crafts, and cannot be left in water that freezes.

Because the only portion of the pipe dock that remains below water is its support network, its environmental impact is almost nil. The width of a pipe dock should be not less than half the height of the structure but can extend much farther out into the water than a floating dock.

Pipe docks are ill-suited for very deep water—about 6 ft. of water is generally accepted as the maximum.

THE PILE DOCK

Wood piles are driven into the lake or riverbed with a pile driver. The dock is secured to the piles.

Pile docks are something of a big brother to pipe docks. Where pipe docks are somewhat limited in that they tend not to work in deep water, pile docks provide the most environmentally friendly permanent solution in relatively deep water (usually, up to 25 ft.), and are limited in size only by local regulations and good taste.

As a general rule, pilings (the large round beams upon which the dock is supported) are stable in all seasons, but severe winter ice can displace pilings and require that they be reset. Like other permanent dock solutions, pile docks are expensive to build, primarily due to the expense in setting the pilings, and more so when they must be set into solid rock (a practice that is not even allowed in some areas).

For these reasons, the do-it-yourself aspect to these docks will largely be confined to the construction of framing and decking once the pilings have been installed by professionals.

THE CRIB DOCK

The dock is supported by a basket built from large timbers and filled with boulders for ballast.

Crib docks rely on underwater cribs containing several tons of stone or concrete and provide the dock with its stability. Crib docks are somewhat more limited than pile docks, but provide a permanent shallow-water (less than 8 ft.) alternative, and can also provide a stable base for a floating dock that attaches to the crib.

What crib docks giveth in stability, they taketh away in environmental impact—they need to be built wide and long for optimal stability (the ratio of height to depth to width is 1-to-1-to-1), so in 6 ft. of water with a $1\frac{1}{2}$ ft. freeboard, you'll need to build a $7\frac{1}{2}$ ft. cube for the crib. In certain circumstances, the sizeable environmental impact of a crib dock (which affects water flows severely) can be a plus: the crib has the ability to break up or divert strong currents, leaving a calm harbor space to one side for mooring and swimming.

Essentially, the crib dock has become a bit of a dinosaur. Many localities have banned them in favor of pile docks, and more are likely to in the future. As DIY projects go, crib docks are not on the list.

Direction of current

A floating dock might seem like a terrible idea for riverfront property. But a floating dock's moorings are more flexible than those of a pipe dock, working by gravity rather than position, so they will always find the bottom while remaining independent of the stabilizing forces for the dock. A floating dock gains its stability from the positioning of the floats, not from its moorings, so it isn't made more or less wobbly by currents.

WHAT DOCK WORKS FOR ME?

Removable dock for strong currents or tides.

A river or stream presents the significant challenge of consistent (and sometimes quite strong) currents, made worse by snow melt, spring ice flows, and debris. Moreover, streams and rivers with fast-moving currents generally have rocky bottoms, not the soft mud that allows the feet of a pipe dock (which could be removed during spring ice flows) to gain the secure foothold needed to keep them in place.

In a strong current, you simply can't store your boat against the current, because this creates a huge surface area for the river to push the boat against the dock, or to pull the dock downstream with it. You'll need to figure out some way to have the boat point straight into the current. For this, you'll need at least one portion of the dock to run parallel to the shore, probably in an L or T shape. A pipe dock is out on this count because there probably isn't

enough friction at the feet to secure the dock, and pipe docks don't break water to create a safe harbor—but floating docks do. When anchored with heavy weights connected by cables to the structure, floating docks depend on gravity rather than bed penetration or friction. This makes them less likely to drift or be pulled downstream by a boat.

Not only are weighted moorings more suitable, they are also independent of the stabilizing forces for the dock: meaning, a floating dock gains its stability from the positioning of the floats, not from its moorings, so it isn't made more or less wobbly by currents. And the floats create a physical barrier to current or ice flow, providing a safe harbor that's conducive to holding a boat in place, particularly in the case of the L-shaped structure.

A pile dock is really the only option for building a dock that's designed for year-round use. As with removable docks, the T or L configuration makes sense when seeking to create an effective harbor for mooring small watercraft. Plan on having your pilings re-driven on a regular basis.

Direction of current

WHAT DOCK WORKS FOR ME?

Permanent dock for rough riverfront.

Because of the immense strength of the pilings on a pile dock, it will maintain its position against the current much more tenaciously than a pipe dock will. On rivers and streams that don't freeze, pilings might be your best dock option, creating a structure that will secure your boat year-round, and will not want to float away.

When used on waterfronts where ice is a factor, a pile dock is still not necessarily out of the question. The problem with a pile dock is money: those pilings don't sink themselves 15 to 40 ft. into the earth. In colder climates, ice flows can (and probably will) uproot your pilings following a normal winter. If you don't mind the likelihood of having your pilings reset professionally, practically on an annual basis, then this is a legitimate and potentially desirable solution.

Crib option: At first glance, a crib dock might seem like the best idea, for no other reason than the fact that it creates a safe harbor to its opposite side. The only problem with the hulking mass that would create such a safe harbor is that it would also serve to catch whatever happens to be floating down the river, particularly debris and silt, which together can negatively affect the ecosystem of your waterfront.

If you set a brick on an incline, and pour sand down that incline, what happens? Some goes to the side, but most of it is caught by the brick. Keep doing that. What you wind up with is much shallower water on the side that breaks the current—much shallower, and a significant alteration in the local ecosystem. For this reason, most regulations on rivers prohibit the construction of crib docks.

A pipe dock is a perfect choice for this, the least challenging of dock sites. Whether you tip it in, flip it in, or roll it in, a pipe dock is inexpensive, easy to build, and lends itself to just about any configuration you like. Pile docks also can work here. Avoid floating docks and crib docks.

WHAT DOCK WORKS FOR ME?

Removable dock for shallow, sandy lakefront.

This is the type of shorefront that will be familiar to many lakefront cabin owners in the American Upper Midwest and Canada, where the lake freezes solid in winter. While the family in this situation would spend a great deal of time both on and in the water, they find themselves frustrated by what the grandkids refer to as the "icky" weeds offshore, and for the same reason, the fishing is very good for vegans, but not too many others.

For shallow, sandy lakefronts, a pipe dock provides an excellent solution with minimal environmental impact. Because the only parts of the dock to touch the water are the support poles, ducks can swim easily underneath the dock and sunlight still gets through to the plantlife below. But best of all, the fact that you can extend a pipe dock well out into the water allows you to build out past those weeds to reach deeper water for swimming, fishing, and boating. Fluctuations in water level can be dealt with by adjusting the leg height, and more significant fluctuations can be easily addressed by moving the dock closer or farther from its current location. Come winter, the pipe dock will be easy to remove in order to avoid the ice that would mangle the whole structure. A roll-in version of the pipe dock is an excellent solution for this type of situation.

A pile dock offers an appealing solution for a shallow, sandy waterfront. Like the pipe dock, the pile dock's only contact with the water is the supports (in this case, pilings). If the lake floor is 6 ft. deep or shallower at the end of the proposed dock, driving piles makes less sense than installing pipes. But if the gradual incline of the lake bed abruptly drops off into deep water, pilings make a bit more sense.

Because of the heft and environmental impact of a crib dock, it is a poor choice for this scenario. Neither is a floating dock a great option, since you need a minimum of 3 ft. of water depth at the shore for the dock to permit appropriate draft beneath it.

A crib dock isn't the best choice for most waterfront properties, but if your local authorities allow them and you don't want to do the work yourself, they are very sturdy structures that withstand rough waters and even create useful harbors.

WHAT DOCK WORKS FOR ME?

Docks for a big body of water with big waves.

One thing is certain: whatever dock you put in the harsh, pounding surf of this waterfront is going to have to take a beating. If your family likes to swim, fish, and boat, a rocky shoreline can be a real impediment. The crashing waves and rocks might provide a nice setting for a particularly depressing Ingmar Bergman movie, but not much else.

Where a floating dock provides some safe harbor in a river current, it becomes a floating safety hazard in strong waves, which can lift your structure out of the water and drop it right back down. A pipe dock would be an absolute disaster in this situation, especially if you intend to moor a boat to it. A tangled mess of wood and pipes will have you putting in a whole new dock continually until you've learned a very valuable, if expensive, lesson—that this was no place for a pipe dock.

A pile dock provides stability and would hold your boat in place securely while giving you access to deeper water for swimming and fishing. The solid rock bottom would make it more difficult/expensive

(and possibly illegal) to drive the piles, however. But still, if your local regulations allow it, a pile dock is probably your best, lowest-impact option. But if your local laws allow crib docks, this would be an ideal place to put one.

In fact, a crib dock, with its giant footprint, tons of rock, and disruption of water flow, is just about as good a solution as one could ask for this rather unfriendly shoreline. Although, as a rule we don't want to alter the ecosystem of the shoreline, sometimes, in order for that shoreline to be remotely serviceable, you're going to need to do some remodeling. Because it is essentially a large pile of rocks encased in lumber, the crib dock creates a safe, calm harbor to the opposite side of its impact point with those strong waves, creating a harbor not unlike the gently lapping waves of a smaller lake. Better still, it provides a much quieter swimming hole for the family, especially when built out into an L or T shape. Crib docks are not for DIYers.

A floating dock is practically the only option for dockbuilding on a very steep or very rocky shoreline. The docks may be anchored with cables attached to submerged weights. Turnbuckles can be used to tighten the cables for holding docks in position.

WHAT DOCK WORKS FOR ME?

Mine-pit lake, deep water, ice floes.

Some lakes are just plain deep. They may not be fraught with threatening waves or even freezing and thawing cycles, but they contain an abundance of water. Choosing a dock type for this situation is pretty simple. You can eliminate crib docks and pipe docks right away because constructing them would not be feasible.

A pile dock would similarly pose significant engineering difficulties, and even if the water was less than 25 ft. deep, the chances are that you'd find yourself paying someone to pound those piles into solid rock, which would make things more expensive than they otherwise would be. So the floating dock is pretty much the only solution for this waterfront.

The difficult part is figuring out how to anchor the floating dock. The best bet in most cases would be anchor weights that rest on the lake bottom and are tethered to the dock with cables and turnbuckles.

WHAT DOCK WORKS FOR ME?

Shallow with gradual decline then steep drop-off.

Certain docks are natural fits with certain shorelines, but what if your scenario is mixed, with a little from Column A, a little from Column B, and maybe a little from Column C? Take, for example, a case where you have nesting ducks at the shore, and a relatively long, shallow decline into the water followed by a steep drop-off. The water level tends to fall somewhat significantly in the course of a year, though not enough to expose a serviceable swath of land to get to a dock built farther out. In scenarios where you have to leapfrog over the shoreline habitat, a pipe dock is a pretty good solution, offering a dock that can be removed in winter, doesn't much disrupt wildlife underneath it, yet can

Combining a run of pipe dock from the shore with a section of floating dock allows you to take advantage of the desirable qualities of pipe docks at the shore, but still extend your dock out into deep water where only floating docks make sense.

easily handle a boat. It would do the same duty here, if only the water didn't become so shallow at times that you cannot bring a boat alongside it. Still, your family would, where possible, like to retain the benefits of the pipe and pile dock to the environment.

A floating dock would be disqualified from the shallow water even if there weren't critters living in those rushes, because the water is usually too shallow to accommodate a floating dock. Still, if you want to be able to park a boat at the dock, there just aren't any other solutions available for the deep water 20 ft. out.

A crib dock is probably out of this equation entirely. A pile dock, on the other hand, would offer many of the benefits provided by the pipe dock, plus greater stability, but at greater expense.

The solution? Since none of these docks solves the riddle alone, but several offer partial answers, we can combine dock types. Essentially, what we need to do is build a bridge out to the floating dock. A pipe dock will provide the smallest environmental footprint over the underwater grasses, so we'll launch with that.

Attaching a floating dock to a pipe dock isn't as simple as hooking up a couple of hinges. Floating docks are heavy and increase draw on the dock, just as if you moored a boat to the dock permanently. One way to reinforce the pipe dock is to build an intermediate transition section between it and the floating dock. If you sink four pilings at the corners of the small transition dock, you will create a sturdy permanent or semi permanent transition. Another possibility is simply to add more pipes to increase the strength, either on the entry dock section or on a smaller transition dock.

Next comes the floating dock. The floating dock is anchored with a series of cables and weights that prevent it from drifting off, but it is also connected to the pile dock with hinges. This way, our fluctuating water levels can be accommodated.

"All of us have in our veins the exact same percentage of salt in our blood that exists in the ocean, and, therefore, we have salt in our blood, in our sweat, in our tears. We are tied to the ocean. And when we go back to the sea—whether it is to sail or to watch it—we are going back from whence we came."

~John F. Kennedy

Tools and Materials

A HUGE PART OF YOUR DOCK-BUILDING SUCCESS HAS TO DO WITH CHOOSING THE RIGHT MATERIALS, AND THIS CHAPTER WILL BE DEVOTED TO EXPLAINING NOT ONLY WHAT THOSE MATERIALS ARE, BUT WHAT MAKES THEM IDEAL FOR THE PURPOSE OF DOCK BUILDING. THIS CHAPTER WILL BREAK DOWN THE BENEFITS AND PITFALLS OF SPECIFIC TOOLS, MATERIALS, AND HARDWARE.

The tools required for the construction (and later maintenance) of a dock are not substantially different than they are for other do-it-yourself projects you've attempted or might attempt. If you think about it, a dock is a relatively simple structure, and so doesn't really require many specialized tools. First things first. For building anything, you'll need:

Pencils. Well, you'll need to mark things. In a pinch, you (and like most of us, probably have) can use anything that leaves a mark—pens, nails, screws, mud, you name it, but believe me, life is a lot easier if you just remember when you check-out at the hardware store to grab a few nice flat carpenter's pencils. They sharpen easily, they're harder to lose than other writing implements, and unlike Junior's No. 2's, you'd have a hard time breaking one in the awkward marking circumstances you'll inevitably create for yourself.

Tape measure(s). The key to all good carpentry is measurement and accurate lines. Really, that's it. If you make a point of keeping your measurements as accurate as is possible, the rest is fairly easy. Get yourself a few good tape measures, and make your life that much easier. A long tape will serve you well for bigger (up to 25 ft.)

measurements, but you may find it a bit cumbersome and awkward for most of the work you'll be doing, so pick up a couple of shorter tapes as well.

Blade. Another must-have for any construction project, the simple utility knife has what seems like a million uses, and one expects a great many more will be discovered in the future.

Tool Belt. Sure you can keep track of your tools, sure you can . . . and with a mouth full of nails or screws, what's not to love? Get yourself a good tool belt—this should provide a series of pockets for the nails, screws, and bolts you'll need for a given task, places for screwdrivers, carpenter's pencil, blade, hammer, drill bits, and, in a perfect world, a holster for your drill/driver.

Level. Levels, if you haven't already discovered, come in all sizes (and increasingly, shapes). Find one at the length you're comfortable with, and this should be good enough for your needs: for example, a 2 ft. aluminum level. A laser level isn't critical, but can be a big help when it comes to leveling dock sections.

Hammer. Since the introduction of the claw, there hasn't been a whole lot of innovation in hammer design. It's a weight with a handle for pounding things. Still, there are things to consider when buying a hammer. First and foremost is its balance. Second is the handle. Recent years have seen the traditional hammer-head on top of wood modi-fied with all sorts of materials, from steel to aluminum to graphite and fiberglass. Some will say that they like the way a wood hammer "bounces back" when compared to a steel han-

dled hammer. Others feel that a steel-handled hammer lands "truer" than its wooden-handled opposite number. It's really a matter of preference.

Saw. Even if you've bought every imaginable cutting implement you've seen in the hardware store, there just isn't a replacement for the good old handsaw for finishing cuts and in tight spots you might be less than eager to share with the irresistible cutting force (and 120 volts of power) of an electric saw.

Screwdrivers.
If there's a theme here, it's that though electric and battery power have saved us a lot of work in recent years, there are times when they are inappropriate or just not feasible. A good set of manually operated screwdrivers is handy for backing bolts, starting screws, and all kinds of things for which your 18-volt drill/driver is more of a hassle or an outright impossibility.

Wrenches. You'll need both a socket set and an open-ended set of wrenches for securing bolts and all manner of dock accessories. For the most part, you'll find yourself needing only the socket set and an adjustable wrench.

Sandpaper. Well, you can't always cut things and leave them. A good file and sanding block will allow you to quickly shave those ugly beards around power-saw cuts.

Circular Saw. This will be the horse for a lot of what you'll be doing. The standard $7\frac{1}{4}$" corded circular saw with a pair of good blades—one for rough cuts and another for finer cuts—will serve pretty much all your needs. Advances in cordless technology have finally lead to cordless circular saws that can cut more than one or two boards in a charge, and they are actually quite useful when doing field work away from a source of electricity.

Cordless Drill/Driver. A good battery-powered drill is something one would assume that anyone seriously considering building his or her own dock probably already has, but with this, as any construction project, a cordless drill is an absolute must-have. A long way from being the weak sister of the electric drill, a good cordless drill (and the emphasis here is on *good*) is everything its electric cousin is and more. If you will be building a very large deck, or at least one with a lot of fasteners, look into picking up a cordless impact driver. These can handle everything from short deck screws to lag screws, and they're usually more lightweight and comfortable to use.

Reciprocating Saw. One of the handiest tools for rough cutting is the reciprocating saw. With the right blade, a reciprocating saw will cut through just about anything. Loaded with a bi-metal blade, it is easily the best field tool for cutting dock poles.

WOOD

Any wood dock you build will face human civilization's perpetual foe—rot. Rot occurs most often where things are neither here nor there, inside or outside, exclusively wet or dry. In the case of a dock, rot tends to occur most often just around the water line, the ebb and flow of which exposes the wood alternately to water and to oxygen, in concert with generally warmer temperatures above the water line, all of which provide an ideal climate for microbes to thrive. I'm sure that if not in person, at the very least in movies, you've seen images of jagged piles jutting out of the water, no longer connected to anything—usually at the same time some creepy music is cued to indicate some unspeakable, impending backwoods horror the wayward city folk are about to encounter.

Naturally resistant outdoor building woods like cedar (above), redwood, and cypress are the best choices for dock framing and decking.

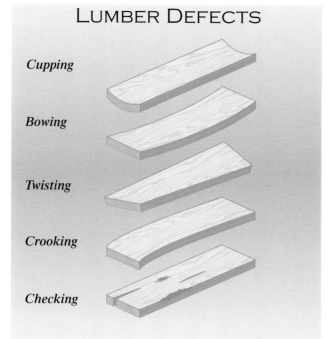

LUMBER DEFECTS

Cupping

Bowing

Twisting

Crooking

Checking

Common wood defects that affect flatness include cupping, bowing, twisting, and crooking. Checks (small crack) and rough edges (wane) degrade both strength and appearance but not flatness.

TIP: If you have the time, hand-select lumber for your deck. Sight down each board to check for bowing and warping. Try to arrange to purchase the wood within a couple of day of the time you'll use it, since it tends to warp or bow as it dries.

So, in creepy movies, who gets out alive? Is it the high-powered advertising executive with his armature of mobile phone, fax machine, business cards, leveraged buyouts, and ability to get a good table at Le Cirque?

No, it's usually the one who, like our backwoods villains, reverts to a near feral state and learns to use

Pressure-treated pine is a popular choice for building docks, and the new-generation products no longer contain arsenic-family chemicals.

nature to combat nature. So too with dockbuilding. To be sure, in the sequel, the protagonist from the first film usually gets it—just as you won't manage to combat rot forever or entirely—but by choosing the right materials, you can have a good run.

Framing and Decking Woods. For the frame and deck, the amount of stress is considerably less than it is for pilings or cribs. Thus, less dense and strong woods with some unique chemical properties are perfectly fine. This is a good thing, too, because the deck and framing are the two items most likely to encounter water and oxygen in just the right amounts to create rot.

The ideal woods for framing and decking are red cedar, redwood and cypress. Like all woods, these contain what are called water soluble phenolics (acidic compounds), which act as preservatives that naturally resist critters and microbes. These woods, in particular, contain much higher concentrations of phenols than other varieties of woods: and they contain them outside their sapwood.

There are few things more breathtaking than new construction of just about anything made of red cedar or redwood. These woods provide a luxurious reddish orange that, given its riotous color, manages to blend into any natural environment in such a way as to make everything around it appear to be so much window dressing. To be sure, red cedar and redwood bespeak a kind of balance between nature and human opulence (a good thing, too, since they are expensive) unparalleled amongst woods.

Like most things, the bright bloom of youth fades to a subtle sort of gray over time. Still, some don't like the natural graying of wood, either

Options for dock decking include pressure-treated pine (A), cedar and other naturally rot-resistant woods (B), composite (C) and plastic, exotic decking such as ipe (D) or teak, and aluminum panels (E).

because they find gray too anonymous or because they believe that wood left to its own devices will rot faster than wood that has been painted or stained.

Pressure-Treated Wood. Well, we were bound to wind up here eventually: the ubiquitous green stuff from which countless docks, decks, children's playgrounds and so forth are constructed. Personally, I find the stuff to be something of a scourge, but within the last couple of years the treating agent has been changed, making it a slightly more appealing option for docks. Because treated pine is the cheapest decking or exterior-rated framing wood you can buy, it is very popular. Structurally, treated posts and framing lumber hold up very well.

TIP: Store framing lumber and wood decking in stacks separated by sticking to allow air flow. It's good to allow the wood to acclimate to the conditions on your property for a couple of days, but try not to let it rest too long, as it can warp or bow.

Plastic and composite decking. The two main types of straight plastic decking are made of PVC (polyvinyl chloride) and PE (polyethylene). PVC (the same stuff used to make plastic fencing and plastic plumbing pipes) is harder than PE, but the PVC chips and cracks more readily. An increasingly practical material for decking is a composite made from wood scraps and (usually) recycled PE. In these, the cellulose structure of the wood is utilized to add two significant things: greater strength and a closer approximation of wood feel. Because wood offers a bit of grit, composites tend to be significantly less slippery than all-plastic decking.

Most PVC decking is one-sided, with the top having a textured plastic surface and the underside consisting of stiffening ribs. Composite decking usually is solid, with the same thickness as wood decking (about 1" actual dimension). Often, the faces have varying degrees of roughness to give you a choice (basically, comfort versus traction). Plastic decking normally has a texture as well, although it's not usually as skidproof as composite. In either case, look for product that has a brushed surface, not an imprinted or embossed surface.

There are some downsides to plastic. The first is that, well, it's plastic—no matter how it's molded or shaped, it still looks like plastic, feels like plastic, and (if you really want to get close) smells like plastic. If you don't like plastic, plastic just isn't going to be your thing, and you'll probably want to stick with wood. If you're like most, and don't mind it one way or the other, then plastic may be a good alternative. Over time, plastic deck boards typically sag; they become brittle in cold temperatures; and they slowly degrade from UV light.

Nonwood decking is growing in popularity. Common options include plastic/wood composite with structural ribs (A), solid composite deckboards with brushed surface (B), structural PVC (C), and FRP (fiberglass reinforced plastic) (D).

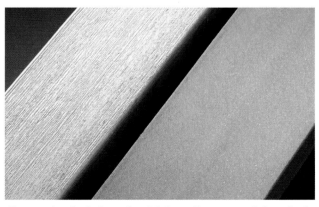

Composite deck boards with heavily textured, brushed surfaces (left) are a better choice than smoother composites (right) because of their anti skid properties.

On the plus side, plastic decking provides superior longevity, flexibility, and ease of maintenance over wood.

Plastic doesn't have the sheer strength to be used in structural parts of your deck, although the industry appears to be closing in on solving the plastic lumber conundrum, probably with a variant of PE plastic or a composite.

METAL

The use of metal in a dock will be largely confined to pipe dock legs, occasionally piles, framing, and connectors (the latter discussed below). Metal allows one to circumvent some of the difficulties encountered with wood structures, of course at a cost. Most metal encountered in do-it-yourself jobs is going to be pre-fabricated, as the welding required tends to be pretty far outside the skill range of DIYers, unless they also happen to be welders.

Steel. Steel oscillates between being a very good choice and a very poor choice, depending on its thickness. It is seldom the prettiest option, primarily

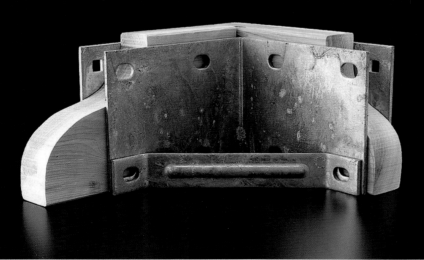

Hot-dipped galvanizing coats plain sheet steel with zinc to cover the dock hardware in a protective layer of zinc. If you will be building your dock from pressure-treated lumber, look for double-dipped or triple-dipped galvanized hardware and fasteners.

due to the fact that it rusts, even if this rust does not cause structural weakness. An ever-so-slightly thicker choice of steel (as little as $\frac{1}{8}$") can mean the difference between a steel structure that rusts through in a few short years, and a structure that will last for many, many years due to the fact that the outer layer of corrosion on thicker steel actually manages to prevent the further intrusion of rust to the structural core.

Galvanized Steel. Given that nobody wants an ugly, rusty-looking dock frame, your choice will probably drift from ordinary steel and toward what is known as hot-dipped galvanized steel. In this process, steel is dipped in a bath of molten zinc, which coats and protects the underlying steel tubing of sheet steel from rust and corrosion. Some might not like the famous dull-silver color of galvanized steel when compared to the bright sheen of virgin steel at installation, but rest assured, a few short months (or weeks, in some applications) will change one's aesthetic appreciation of naked steel.

Double-dipped and triple-dipped galvanized steel is steel that is given the hot zinc bath two or three times. The coating of zinc is thicker and the protection offered by the double dipping is longer lasting than that provided by a single dip. Especially important if you are building with treated lumber: look for triple-dipped parts and hardware. One of the surprises delivered in the switch from old CCA lumber to ACQ and copper azole is that both new compounds cause excessive corrosion when they react with the zinc in galvanized steel. Galvanized steel can be painted, and should definitely be painted if it will be used in salt water, as salt water has an ability to corrode the zinc coating. To paint galvanized steel, all grease needs to be removed from the zinc coating, and what is known as an etching primer should be applied, which provides both a secure bond to the zinc surface, and surface that the top coat can more easily bond to.

Powder and Spray Coatings. In recent years, these have gained significantly in popularity, though their durability still lags somewhat behind the aforementioned coatings. In these coatings, the metal is heated beyond the melting point of the coating, and dipped in or sprayed with a vinyl or PE powder that then melts to the surface of the metal on contact. These provide a nice, smooth, and aesthetically pleasant surface, and often contain pigments, so the final coating resembles a well-painted surface.

Stainless Steel. Well, this would be the best choice for everything on a dock but the decking—if you had an unlimited budget. Stainless steel is an alloy with a high nickel and chromium content that gives it its attractive shiny silver appearance and near-imperviousness to rust and other afflictions. Stainless, in spite of its cost, is sometimes the only

Powder-coated steel is the material of choice for economy-grade deck hardware. Avoid scratching it and exposing the raw steel below the painted surface.

choice for certain salt-water applications. For fresh-water applications, the difference in cost is fairly minimal for things that would be subject to our old friends a little moisture and a little oxygen, such as dock ladders. Stainless steel is an attractive alternative to wood in these cases. Otherwise, it is likely that you would only want to use stainless steel on visible brackets and connections, not necessarily for reasons of utility, but for aesthetics.

Aluminum. Aluminum doesn't rust and provides a reasonably strong and very lightweight alternative for dock applications. Aluminum needs to be thicker than steel because it is a weaker metal, but even in thicker sizes, it remains lighter than steel. Aluminum is significantly more expensive than hot-dipped steel, but where removal of the dock is necessary to avoid mangling by ice, it is an expensive convenience that's easy to justify.

Aluminum creates its own protection. The outer layer of aluminum (if properly exposed) creates a thin coating of oxidization when exposed to the elements, which prevents its structural core from

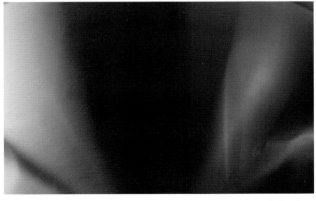

Stainless steel is a premium metal for structural dock parts because it is highly resistant to rust and corrosion and it retains its strength. But it is the most expensive dock material available.

Structural aluminum is strong, lightweight, and moisture resistant. It's used commonly as a building material for roll-in docks, boat hoists, and decking panels.

corroding. Problems do occur with aluminum, particularly at connections, because the aluminum is not sufficiently exposed to the elements to form its protective coating. Aluminum can experience similar and more severe problems in salt water, due largely to the fact that salt water conducts electricity more efficiently than does fresh water. Thus, when aluminum is connected to dissimilar and reactive metals, such as (nonstainless) steel, the two metals tend to corrode one another. For this reason, try to pair like with like (aluminum with aluminum) or aluminum with a nonreactive metal such as stainless steel.

DOCK HARDWARE

Most DIY docks are made from kits of varying level of completeness. At the very least, the dock sections are typically held together by some kind of engineered system of connectors. You can purchase elaborate systems of proprietary parts, which are typically not interchangeable. Or you can buy a simpler system of similar-looking parts that are probably not interchangeable among manufacturers.

Like any exterior metal parts, dock hardware should be resistant to corrosion and rust. If you build a dock in detachable sections, then you don't want the bolts connecting those sections to corrode and become immovable, necessitating the removal of their connectors to take the dock apart. Wherever possible, buy hardware made specifically for marine applications, purchased from a dock building supplier with some good history.

It is possible to build a dock without using any specialty dock hardware. There isn't necessarily any problem with that, especially if you're building a dock that doesn't require seasonal removal. But in just about any case you'll be better off taking advantage of the engineering that went into creating corner brackets, sleeves, and other hardware.

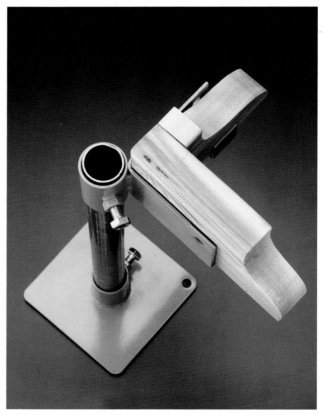

Specialty dock hardware makes dock building easier and, when used correctly, guarantees that your dock will be structurally sound.

Corner Brackets. If you've ever tried stacking boxes on their sides, you'll have some understanding of why corner brackets are needed. From boats banging into your dock, to the more firm anchoring at the shore competing with the less firm anchoring in the water—corners like to collapse when given the chance. Thus, no matter how skilled you may be as a joiner, for an application such as a dock you will need to use corner brackets.

Corner brackets come in two varieties: those that fit inside the frame of your dock, and those that fit outside. Generally speaking, unless your dock is particularly large and thus in need of added support, you won't require outside corner brackets. Thus, what you'll need are good solid inside corner brackets, and ideally corner brackets that provide cross-bracing to distribute the stress across as much space as is possible.

Hinges. Hinges may prove necessary in cases where you include a ramp, or need to connect a nonfloating portion of a dock to a floating portion to accommodate fluctuating water levels. Hinges prevent the connected portions of the dock from moving from side to side, but facilitate smooth movement up and down. It should be noted that hinges are not to be used to connect two floating sections to one another. Some pricier options encase the pins in nylon to cut down on squeakiness.

DOCK HINGES

This hot-dipped galvanized hinge is secured with a cotter pin that is removed when you take the dock in for the winter.

This powder-coated dock hinge allows limited up-and-down movement between two adjoining dock sections or between a dock section and an on-shore deck or launching pad.

Dock sections are held together with hinged connectors so they adjust (or can be manually adjusted) to rising and falling water levels. The basic dock hinge is a metal plate with a cylinder that mounts to one dock section. The cylinder fits into an access hole in a plate that mounts to the adjoining dock section. They are installed in pairs. Dock-building kits usually employ custom-designed hinging devices that are designed to work with their dock undercarriage hardware.

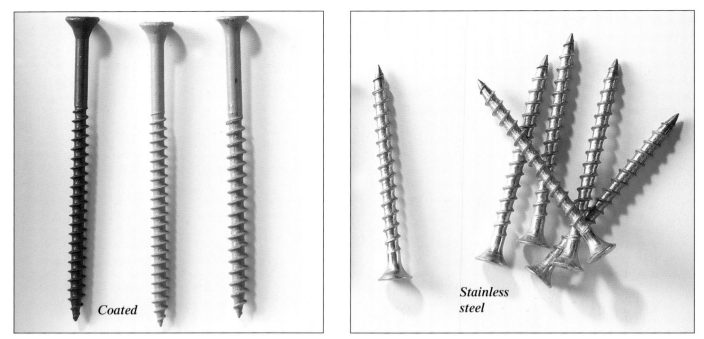

Deck screws are used to attach deck boards to the dock frame, but should not be relied upon as the sole connectors for joining framing members. Coated (left) or stainless-steel (right) deck screws hold up better than cheaper types. Use 2½" screws to fasten ⁵⁄4 deck boards. Use 3" screws to fasten 2× decking.

Carriage bolts, lag bolts, and lag screws are used to fasten structural framing members for docks. Choose hot-dipped galvanized (triple-dipped if you're using pressure-treated lumber) or stainless steel.

Hinges, which connect sections with a simple pin threaded through sockets, should make for an easy tear-down at season's end and painless reassembly in spring through the removal or replacement of the pins.

Connectors. Connectors are similar to hinges, but along with preventing the lateral movement of the dock sections, they prevent vertical movement as well. Think of them as very poorly designed hinges—instead of providing a single pin that pivots, connectors usually have two or more pins to prevent such pivoting. The same rules apply for inserting and removing the pins as they do for hinges, however. You should be able to easily remove and replace pins as needed for assembly and disassembly. At the same time, when pins are in place, you want to have as little movement as possible, thus allowing you to connect smaller sections of dock to create one very stable whole. Any give at the anchor

PAINT & STAIN

A well-maintained paint or sealing job on your dock will protect it against rot. However, you would do well to consider that a dock surface handles a lot more activities than does the side of a house. From the everyday dropping and dragging of things on or across its surface, including chairs, anchors, fishing gear, and so forth, to seasonal ice and snow, not to mention the inevitable swelling and shrinking that will outstrip the swelling and shrinking of anything you paint the surface with, you start to get an idea. If you combine ice, weather, and daily activity, you'll find that it isn't easy to maintain a painted surface in the dock's environment. If you decide to paint, you'll have to figure on constant vigilance of your painted or stained surface, and redoing the whole thing every couple years.

You can obtain a colored surface but minimize the maintenance by choosing a penetrating deck stain. Although they are designed for decks, penetrating stains won't achieve their longevity claims on a wood dock simply because the nature of the forces working against them is quite different on docks. Always apply them to the dock boards when they are on shore, and look for a product that offers protection from UV rays.

Polyurethane and other film-forming wood finishes should be avoided on docks. You can use marine varnish to apply a layer of clear protection to the dock boards, but the main outcome of using this product will be a slippery dock. And even marine-grade varnish will blister and peel on an annual basis, resulting in very significant maintenance.

Semitransparent deck stain is a good choice if you decide to stain your dock. Plan on stripping and restaining your dock annually (preferably on shore).

point will encourage rot and corrosion of metals. If, in demolishing something, you've ever extracted a bolt with a crowbar, this should give you an idea—a little opening, wiggle it, keep going until the metal weakens and breaks off.

Fasteners. Deck screws are pretty much all coated in this day and age (usually lightly galvanized), but you might find that spending the extra money here for an epoxy or ceramic coating is well worth it. Though pricey in larger applications, the cost won't be terribly prohibitive in this application, and the ceramic and epoxy coatings will far

outlast galvanized coatings or heat-tempered finishes common on cheap deck screws.

Bolts. Lag bolts, lag screws, and carriage bolts are the glue that hold many dock frames together. Don't skimp on these items. For structural members, never use anything less that $1/2$" dia. bolts. Stainless steel is best, but you may also use hot-dipped galvanized bolts (the electroplated cheapies are virtually useless outdoors).

Removable docks should be modular in nature to make them easier to get in and out of the water. The carpentry technique required to make modular dock sections essentially involves building a series of small decks.

BUILDING DOCK SECTIONS

NO MATTER WHICH SUPPORT SYSTEM YOU CHOOSE FOR YOUR WOOD DOCK, BE IT FLOATING, PIPE, PILE, CRIB, OR HERD OF TURTLES, ONE CONSTRUCTION ASPECT REMAINS PRETTY MUCH STANDARD ACROSS THE BOARD: FRAMING AND DECKING.

Building a sturdy frame and attaching decking represent the lion's share of the carpentry work for most DIY dock building. The same can be said of building a land deck as well, but there are important differences between docks and decks. Where decks are joined with screws, bolts, and lumber hanger hardware, the method for joining and reinforcing dock frames varies depending on the type. Pipe docks, for example, are built with corner connectors that have integral pipe sleeves. Since many of these

connectors are based on unique fastening systems, how you put your dock together can vary quite a bit. As with decks, fasteners and hardware for aquatic use must be resistant to rust and corrosion.

In this chapter we'll show you some basic information on building a wood support frame for a dock section and how to install decking onto the frame. Then, we'll present some sequences of actual dock section construction.

PARTS OF A DOCK DECK

Header. At the outermost end of the dock, the header is the starting point. On a simple, rectangular shape, the header makes the short sides of the rectangle. Usually you will reserve 2 × 8" boards for your headers. Use the straightest lumber in your pile for this purpose, as well as for outside stringers to help in your effort to create angles as close to 90° as possible.

Stringers. Generally, stringers are the sides of the dock frame and also the intermediate members that run between the front and back header to support decking. Though it is not absolutely essential that internal stringers be perfectly straight, it helps. The stringers that form the outer portion of your frame should be selected because they are straight.

Crossers. Crossers provide additional side-to-side structural support, and are placed beneath stringers in docks built from scratch using traditional dock-building techniques.

Decking. Where boards for the structural members should be straight, with decking it's a beauty contest. Bowed, warped, or crooked decking boards can be worked around, but ugly, scarred, knotted, or otherwise flawed members will make up what you'll be looking at for pretty much the life of the dock.

Skirt. A skirt is not an essential part of the dock, but it creates a surface that won't gouge boats or the hands and legs of swimmers. Besides that, it just looks nice, especially if the ends of your decking are deteriorating.

BUILDING DOCK SECTIONS: THE BASIC RECTANGLE

For starters, let's build a simple rectangular frame. It could be any size, really, but if you'll be installing and removing the dock every year, limit the sizes of the sections to no bigger than 4 ft. by 10 ft. Local regulations likely will limit the total width and length of the dock.

The parts of a dock are very similar to the parts of a deck. Unless you have an unlimited supply of perfect boards to work with, prioritize a bit when you select your lumber for each dock part. Choose straight boards (likely 2 × 8 stock) to make your headers and stringers. If the board crowns from bowing, orient it with the convex edge facing up. Cut the headers and stringers to length with a power miter saw or circular saw and straightedge cutting guide. Arrange the boards on a flat surface to form a rectangle. Tack the rectangle together temporarily with one screw per joint.

Once you've tacked the frame together, check it for square. One method is to measure from one corner diagonally to the opposite corner, then take the other diagonal measurement. If your two diagonal measurements are identical, you've created a perfect rectangle. For smaller frames, you can simply use a carpenter's square. Once you've determined the frame is square, you can drive all of the remaining corner screws according to your fastener schedule.

Install the intermediate stringers inside the frame. For 2× decking, place the stringers no more than 24" apart on-center. For $\frac{5}{4}$ deck boards (actual thickness is 1"), the stringers should be placed no more than 16" apart on-center. If you will be using plastic decking, then you'll need to consult the manufacturer's literature for structural needs to support that particular decking. In other words, if you are building a 4-ft.-wide dock, you'll need a pair of evenly spaced intermediate stringers to support $\frac{5}{4}$ decking, while one stringer right down the middle will suffice to support 2× decking (usually 2 × 6).

On the header, mark *both* sides of the header with a rectangle with an "X" through it to indicate the stringer position. This makes it easier to find the stringer when screwing your decking in place. Measure, cut, and verify the length of all stringers and then attach them inside the frame at the marked locations using deck screws.

Unless you're building a floating dock or a dock that will be in shallow water, you can increase the rigidity of the structure by adding cross support underneath the stringers. These "crossers" will help minimize sag in the dock platform. Flip the structure over and prepare to install crossers. Crossers will be the same length as your headers but can be taken from the worst wood in your pile. Using the

same method you used for preparing to install stringers, mark the outside stringers as though they were headers above. Because another purpose of crossers is to maintain equal distance between stringers at all points, this might be a time for using your pipe clamp. Pull any unruly stringers to their correct measurement with the pipe clamp or just your hand if they aren't terribly bent. Attach the crossers to the stringers with two screws per joint,

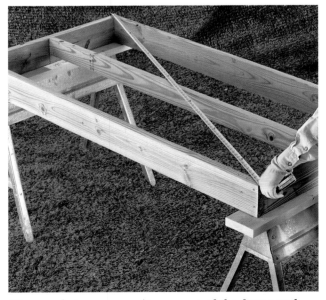

Measure between opposite corners of the frame and compare the measurements to determine if the frame is square. This is called "Measuring the diagonals."

unless your crossers are larger than 2 × 4, in which case you should add a screw for every extra 2".

Now that you have a nice solid frame, it's time to make it more solid. Install your corner and stringer brackets at this time. Because you were careful to mark both sides of the wood, drilling holes for your brackets should be relatively easy, but make certain that your drill holes are very perpendicular. You can purchase right-angle guides for your drill to ensure that your holes will be perpendicular. Once you've solidified your solid frame, with its perfect angles and such, it's time to dress it up.

INSTALLING DECKING

Now you're ready to install your decking. There are many ways to go about this. The most basic is simply to attach the deck boards directly to the stringers in a nice, straight row. The only drawback to this simple solution is that it makes for a heavy dock section that will probably require multiple people to take in and put out. For this reason, the decking is often attached to runners in small sections. The sections are friction-fitted into the frame so they can be removed and installed easily, leaving only the frame itself to be moved and leveled. The pipe dock project featured on pages 75 to 81 employs this kind of a system.

When you cut your deck boards to length, oversize them a couple of inches if you can. Instead of painstakingly aligning the board ends as you go, install them with a bit of overhang on each end. Then, when all the deck boards are in, you can clamp a straightedge to the section and cut them to length all at once with a circular saw. If you're pretty handy with a trim saw, you might be able to do a good job simply flush-cutting the ends to the frame.

HOW TO BUILD A DOCK FRAME

1 *Cut the headers and stringers to length and tack the frame together with one deck screw per joint. Check the frame for squareness by measuring the diagonals (see previous page).*

2 *Attach a pair of 2 × 6 crosspieces to the underside of the frame to hold the frame members together and maintain square corners.*

3 *Attach corner brackets to each corner. The exact style of corner bracket will depend on what type of dock you're building (pipe dock or floating dock). Clamp the brackets to the frame and then secure them with the recommended fasteners.*

You won't want to screw your decking planks in snug to one another. Instead, make sure there are small gaps between planks so a little sunlight and air can get through. Gaps also permit runoff and they allow for swelling of the wood. Use spacers to set even gaps. A small screwdriver shank works well, as does a 10d common nail.

Strategies vary on the best place to start installing decking. How you go about it depends on whether you have the equipment and the inclination to rip any of the deck boards for width. If you'd just as soon work with whole boards, the easiest technique is to install the deck boards at each end of the dock section first and then dry-fit the intermediate boards. Lay as many as you can fit into the area between the ends, trying to maintain a small gap between each pair of boards. Once the space is filled, adjust the spacing using trial and error until your eye tells you that they are relatively even and the gaps are no more than $\frac{1}{2}$" wide. Then create a spacer that's the same thickness as the gap.

As you install the deck boards, be sure to drill pilot holes for the deck screws, at least where they attach to the outside stringers (with softwood you can probably get by without pilot holes for the intermediate stringers, but you'll always get a neater result with less splintering if you drill a pilot.) Use a portable drill or cordless drill/driver to drive the deck screws. Drive them until the heads are slightly countersunk, taking care not to overdrive (this weakens the holding power and creates deeper holes for water to collect in).

Invariably, your pretty wood won't all be straight, but because you've built such a nice, solid structure underneath, you don't need to worry. There are methods for returning crooked boards to the straight and narrow path.

Drill pilot holes for deck screws, especially when driving screws near the ends or edges of deck boards. For typical deck screws, a $\frac{1}{8}$" drill bit is recommended.

Drive two screws through each deck board at each joist location. For $\frac{5}{4}$ deck boards, use $2\frac{1}{2}$" screws; for 2× decking, use 3" screws.

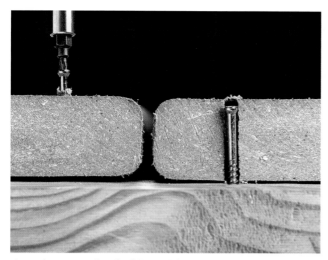

Attach composite decking with self-tapping composite screws. These specially designed screws limit the "mushroom" effect that often occurs with standard deck screws (the screw forces material up into a mushroom shape around the edges of the screwhole).

The first method for straightening a board is to use a pipe clamp. First, you'll need to attach the deck board anywhere you can create a proper gap. Then fasten one end of the pipe clamp to the header, tighten the other end at the crooked board, drawing it back into a straight line with the other, better-behaved decking planks. This method, of course, is done if the gap is too wide because of bowing. Once you have it drawn back far enough (remember your spacers), screw the plank into position.

The second method is a bit more low tech, and perhaps a bit more cumbersome, but works in situations where the gap is either too wide or too narrow. By inserting a pry bar into a gap that's too narrow, you can force the deck boards apart the proper amount and then drive your deck screws. For extra wide gaps, tack a bracing board to the stringers next to the bowed board and use the pry bar to lever the bowed board toward its neighbor.

For a more finished appearance, and to minimize the exposure of the end grain on the deck boards, cut and attach skirt boards to the dock section. Usually

As you near the end of a run (within four to six boards) dry-lay deck boards up to the end to see where the layout will end up relative to the rim joist. If the last board comes up just a little bit short of the outside edge of the joist, you may be able to accommodate by increasing the spacing between boards slightly. If the last board overhangs the rim joist, use the dry layout to determine how much material needs to be rip cut.

Use a flat pry bar to force bowed deck boards into alignment. If the gap between boards is too small, drive the pry bar into the gap until your spacer (a 10d nail, for example) fits in, and then screw the board at the joist and move on to the next one. If the gap is too large, tack a wood block to the joist below the edge of the deck board and use the block as a fulcrum to leverage the board into position.

Trim the ends of the installed deck boards flush with the outer stringers. If you are handy with a trim saw, you can probably freehand this cut. Otherwise, clamp a straightedge cutting guide to the dock deck.

For a more finished appearance, frame the dock sections with 1× or 2× lumber, mitered at the corners, to create skirting.

made with choice 1× stock, skirt boards can be butted or mitered together. Mitered corners look more professional (at first anyway) but they are also more prone to opening and creating gaps.

As you can see, building a basic dock isn't that complicated. It simply requires selecting the proper woods for each part, careful measurement, and rechecking your measurements. With any support system, the dock above would serve (if large enough) most any purpose the average watergoing family might require. The thing about dock building is that just about anything, any crazy style you can think of, will ultimately make use of exactly what you just learned.

MORE TIPS FOR WORKING WITH COMPOSITE AND PLASTIC DECKING

Tongue-and-groove style composite decking is installed in much the same manner as wood tongue-and-groove strip flooring. Begin with a starter strip that has a groove facing outward, and fill in by inserting the tongues of the adjoining strip into the groove. Attach strip through the groove flanges.

Leave a ⅛" gap between deck boards that are butted together end-to-end. Make sure this joint falls over a stringer. For most docks, you're not likely to encounter this situation except when trying to stretch the materials by using cutoff pieces to span relatively short distances.

Some plastic and composite decking is secured with T-clips or other fasteners that allow you to attach the boards without marring the surfaces, creating a smooth, neat installation.

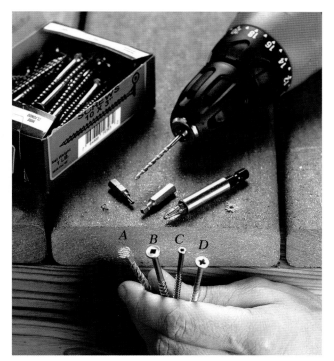

Acceptable fasteners for attaching composite and plastic decking include exterior-rated spiral-shank nails (A), stainless-steel deck screws (B), self-tapping composite deck screws (C), and coated deck screws (D).

Decking pattern variation: Diagonal
A diagonal deck board layout pattern is relatively easy to install and, for this reason, not uncommon to find on a dock. This pattern will increase the cost of the dock, however, since the stringers need to be closer together than with a standard layout.

Decking pattern variation: Diamonds
A series of diamonds evokes the idea of parquet flooring. The effect can be very dramatic on a dock, but if your dock section is less than 4 ft. wide it probably will look strange. Requiring doubled stringer with doubled blocking in between, the pattern is among the more time consuming to install.

Decking pattern variation: Knockout
If you fish off your dock you might appreciate this idea: Frame an opening in the dock and create a removable decking cover. The opening gives you a sheltered spot for storing bait buckets or catch baskets in the water. Do not leave the hole uncovered when not in use.

Decking pattern variation: Border
Another pattern that has high visual drama is to create a border to frame a field of dock boards, often installed on the diagonal. Although this also won't work on narrower docks, it's a fun way to dress up a platform (such as a swimming raft).

"Chance is always powerful. Let your hook be always cast; in the pool where you least expect it, there will be a fish."
~ Ovid (43 BC – 17 AD)

BUILDING PIPE DOCKS

T HE PIPE DOCK (ALSO CALLED THE POLE DOCK)
IS PROBABLY THE MOST COMMON TYPE OF
DOCK, PARTICULARLY FOR INLAND LAKES
AND RIVERS WHERE WINTER REMOVAL IS REQUIRED.
THE BASIC SETUP INVOLVES DRIVING GALVANIZED
METAL PIPES INTO THE LAKE OR RIVER BOTTOM (OR
STABILIZING THEM ON WIDE FEET IN SOFTER BEDS),
AND THEN CLAMPING THE DOCK SECTIONS TO THE
PIPES IN ADJUSTABLE PIPE SLEEVES. IN ADDITION
TO BEING QUITE SIMPLE TO BUILD, A PIPE DOCK
IS ALSO THE CHEAPEST TYPE OF DOCK YOU CAN
MAKE YOURSELF.

*The basic pipe dock is easy, inexpensive, and suitable for a variety of lake
and river beds, making it extremely popular.*

In the basic pipe dock design, metal pipe sleeve hardware is mounted to the outside faces of the dock frame. For the corners, you use inside or outside corner brackets, often with integral pole sleeves. On the sides of the stringers between corners, the sleeve has a flat mounting plate that you attach. A set screw (actually, a bolt in most cases) in the sleeve secures it to the pipe once the pipe is slipped through the sleeve and the height is set.

Although it isn't always used and may not be necessary in some cases, metal crossbracing that spans the legs lends sturdiness to any pipe dock. The crossbracing may be installed during construction of the dock sections or during installation.

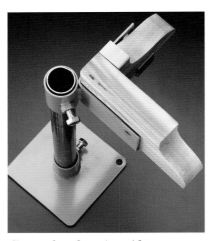

Corner brackets (outside corner shown) with integral pipe sleeves are the backbone of a pipe dock.

On shore and in lakes or rivers with a solid earth bed, you can simply drive the pipes home with a sledge until they are in solidly.

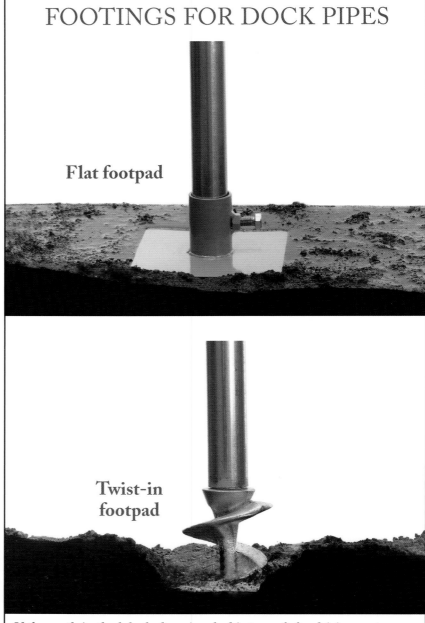

FOOTINGS FOR DOCK PIPES

Flat footpad

Twist-in footpad

If the earth in the lake bed or river bed is too soft for driving posts, your options include attaching a flat footpad to the bottom of the pipe (top) or twist-in footpads (bottom).

See the chapter on installing pipe docks (pages 102 to 104) for more information on crossbracing, as the specific type you select may affect the construction sequences for your dock.

Pipe docks resemble pile docks in that the support for the decking is a series of legs that rest on the floor of a body of water. Unlike the pile dock, in which piles are driven into the ground beneath the water, and remain where driven, the pipe dock is removable, and depends on gravity to remain in place.

Pipe docks can be adjusted fairly easily to reset your desired freeboard distance as the level of the water rises and falls. In most cases, adjusting the height of the dock is simply a matter of loosening the bolt that secures the sleeve around each pipe and then lowering or raising the dock platform. Use a level to make sure the dock is level and safe each time you make an adjustment.

Pipe docks can provide mooring for smaller watercraft, but only for short periods of time in calm water. The spindly pipes simply won't hold up against the strong forces that can be applied by a larger craft yearning to be set free. By increasing the

HOW TO BUILD A PIPE DOCK

1 Cut 2 × 6 headers and stringers to length using a circular saw or a power miter saw on a stand. Also cut the 2 × 4 center stringer 3" shorter than the outside stringers.

2 Lay out the 2 × 6 stringer end locations and the 2 × 4 center stringer location onto the headers. Gang the headers together edge to edge with the ends flush and mark them at the same time, using a carpenter's square as a guide.

3 *Tack the boards together (two headers, two outside stringers, and one center stringer) by driving a couple of deck screws at each joint. The center stringer should be flush with the top edges of the outside stringers, not the bottom edges. Test the corners with a carpenter's square as you work.*

4 *Take diagonal measurements between opposite corners. If the measurements are equal, it means the dock frame is square. If not, apply counter pressure to the corners to shift the frame into square. Drive additional deck screws at each joint to secure them in a square position.*

number, size, and depth of the pipes you can beef up the dock's resistance to forces that seek to uproot it. But for a more permanent solution, install an adjoining boat lift with a hoist so you can get the craft out of the water when not in use.

The spindliness of the pipes may be a disadvantage when it comes to resisting currents, but it is an advantage environmentally. The only part of a pipe dock that is submerged is the support network, which leaves a relatively clear path for waterflow and requires only minimal disruption of the lake bed or river bed. If your shoreline is environmentally sensitive (for example, a nesting place for loons), a pipe dock is a good choice (although a different location should be your first choice).

Pipe docks should be a minimum of 3 ft. in width. The length is limited only by local codes and your water depth: pipe docks should not be installed in water that's more than 6 ft. deep.

Many pipe docks, including the one seen here, feature removable decking that simplifies seasonal installation and removal. Most pipe-dock hardware will support decking that is installed in sections with decking that can be removed in manageable sections. Building removable decking for your dock isn't so mysterious a process. Like most everything on your dock, this involves good measurement and rudimentary physics. Even if you don't remove your dock in winter, removable panels make any unscheduled maintenance and adjustments to the framing an easier matter altogether.

Removable panels are built in such a way that decking sits on runners that work in conjunction with additional structural features of your dock, rather than being individual planks nailed into the framing,

In essence, your frame provides a cradle into which the decking fits. Just as with permanent decking, the decking members are supported as required by the variety of decking you've chosen. Another benefit to this decking scheme is that you can fasten the deck boards from the bottom, rather than the top, leaving a nice, pristine deck free of the blight of screwholes.

5 *Attach a deck board at each end of the frame. The edges of the deck board should be flush with the outside faces of the deck frame. Use three 2½" galvanized, coated, or stainless-steel deck screws at each stringer (including the center one).*

6 *To help keep the frame from racking, attach a deck board to the underside of the frame at each end. Driving a few screws through the deck board and into the header will further stiffen the structure.*

USING STOCK HARDWARE

While specialty dock hardware makes building docks practically foolproof, it certainly is possible to build a dock using only conventional building materials (specialty hardware always increases project prices). If you choose to rely on your own creativity and resourcefulness to solve dockbuilding issues, you should still attempt to use metal hangers and braces as much as possible. These products (like the corner brackets shown here) are relatively inexpensive and they create corners and joints that hold up better to water and shrinking and swelling than joints that are made with fasteners alone. Just be sure to buy stainless-steel or triple-dipped galvanized hangers and brackets.

Attach the metal hangers and brackets with hot dipped joist hanger nails, or other hot-dipped galvanized common nails (usually 10d) as specified in the fastening schedule for the hardware (check the hanger hardware catalog at the store where you purchase the materials). See Resources, page 124.

7 Attach the pole sleeves according to the manufacturer's instructions. Generally, sleeves should be flush with the tops of the stringers and headers, 1½" from ends that will not connect with other dock section, as in the inset photo. Use four 5/16" × 2½" hot-dipped galvanized or stainless-steel carriage bolts for each sleeve. Hinged post sleeves like the one in the main photo above usually are positioned with their edge flush against the outside of the header. This may require you to use 4" or 5" lag screws instead of carriage bolts to attach the sleeve.

When employing a removable decking approach, the arrangement of the stringers may need to be reoriented. In some applications, the stringers must go in the direction of the headers because the point of contact for the removable decking works best when it is at 90° angles to the stringers. Thus, in a perfect world, its runners rest on the stringers, distributing the weight of the decking and fat Uncle Lou across the whole structure, rather than individually. But in other cases, including the demonstration dock shown on these pages, the frame of the dock section is similar in construction to the one built on pages 62 to 73.

2 × 4 Runner

8 Build the decking insert so the deck boards are evenly spaced and the outside faces of the runners are spaced according to your plan (32½" apart as shown here). Use two or three deck screws at each runner. When the decking track is done, insert it into the frame to test the fit and adjust if needed. If you prefer not to see any exposed screwheads, attach the decking to the runners by driving screws up through the runners.

Permanently attached to dock frame

Panel on runner

Runner

Panel on runner

Deck boards removed for clarity

Panel on runner

9 Assemble all of your deck parts and test the hardware to make sure everything fits together as planned. The panels do not require direct fastening to the dock frame. They are supported by the outer and middle stringers. If a panel feels loose inside the frame, however, you may want to drive a couple of short deck screws through the runners and into the frame to hold it in place.

BUILDING FLOATING DOCKS

FLOATING DOCKS ARE ONE OF THE MOST COMMON AND VERSATILE TYPES OF DOCK FOR RESIDENTIAL USE. THEY ARE CALLED FLOATING DOCKS NOT BECAUSE THE DOCK DECK ITSELF IS BUOYANT, BUT BECAUSE THEY UTILIZE FLOATS THAT ARE MOUNTED TO THE UNDERSIDE OF THE DOCK FRAME TO SUPPORT THE DOCK. THIS MAKES THEM VERY USEFUL FOR SEASONAL REMOVAL AND EASILY THE BEST OPTION FOR INSTALLING A DOCK IN DEEP WATER. THIS CHAPTER WILL LOOK AT DIFFERENT FLOATATION MECHANISMS, INCLUDING SOME THINGS YOU WILL NEED TO AVOID.

Floating docks are held up by heavy-duty plastic floats that are attached to the underside of the dock. Some floats are hollow, but the better ones are filled with nonabsorbent foam. Floating docks must be anchored securely with cables and weights or attached to a permanent structure.

FLOATING DOCKS AND STABILITY

A floating dock's stability has to do first with the ability of the chosen floatation device to maintain a consistent freeboard (support the weight above it—including fat Uncle Lou), and the positioning of the floats. To accomplish this, you want to choose something that will be able to support the weight you put on it. Though a piece of driftwood may float, it isn't something you'd like to stand on. To start thinking about positioning, consider the difference between a canoe and a pontoon boat. In a canoe, any noncounterbalanced weight put to any of the edges will tip the whole thing. If you are on a pontoon boat, by contrast, you can step wherever you want and still feel a nice, stable surface underfoot.

This latter point may seem somewhat obvious, but I'm sure you've stepped on your share of seemingly well-built but wobbly docks, so evidently it isn't obvious enough to everyone. When placing your floats, you'll want to place them as close as possible to the outside of the dock. It may look nicer to have your floats set back a bit

DOCK FLOATS

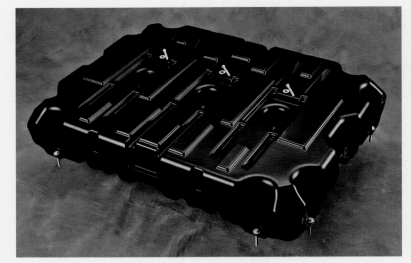

This plastic float measures 9 × 36 × 48" and has a buoyancy rating of 500 pounds. At approximately $70 it is very economical, but like other inexpensive floats it is completely hollow. It is attached to the dock undercarriage with lag screws and washers.

Dock floats are attached to the underside of your dock deck to hold it up. A properly sized float, on average, will be submerged roughly halfway into the water when the dock is in use. Typically, a dock will have several floats to distribute the load. Most floats today are made from heavy-duty plastic, often HDPE. The cheaper ones (above) are hollow. Better-quality floats (below) are filled with nonabsorbent foam, such as EPS, so they don't fill up with water immediately if they develop a leak. For information on repairing a float, see page 120.

These commercial-grade floats are filled with foam so they do not fill up with water immediately if they form a leak. They are considerably more expensive than the consumer models.

underneath the dock where they are mostly invisible, but you sacrifice some stability.

The next rule of floatation is size. The bigger the dock, the more stable the dock will be—if stepping on one side of a dock acts as a lever, then figure it is much more difficult to pull up a heavier object than a smaller one—if you ever tried to see-saw with someone much bigger than you, you'd have an idea. Greater surface area means that the dock will have greater weight, and will be less likely to tip.

While a giant dock would be more stable than a smaller one, most don't find blotting out all the water on their shoreline an appealing option. Fortunately, there are ways to use physics to offset the lack of an enormous structure. The most obvious is to increase the weight of the dock by other means, such as a heavy subframe or anchor weights. In such applications, it of course becomes necessary to increase the amount of floatation.

An important aspect of designing a floating dock is choosing the floats you'll use. Independent of quality (we'll discuss that in a bit), you need to determine exactly how much work your floats will need to do. This is expressed as a minimum buoyancy rating. Calculating buoyancy requirements can get a bit tricky. For you left-brain people out there, it's force

MINIMUM BUOYANCY REQUIREMENTS

Residential dock:
25 to 30 lbs. per sq. ft.
Oversize or commercial dock:
30 to 40 lbs. per sq. ft.

Example: A 4 × 10-ft. dock has an area of 40 sq. ft. For a residential dock, that means floats must have total rated buoyancy of 40 times 25, which equals 1,000 pounds per square foot. To adequately support the load, a dock of this size would need, for example, two of the 500-pound rated floats seen on the previous page.
Note: This information is for estimating purposes only. Confirm your floatation requirements with your dock-materials retailer before purchasing floats.

(total live load plus dead load) divided by area and halved. Making specific calculations for your dock will yield the most accurate results, but to avoid the work and confusion, simply multiply the total square footage of the dock surface times 25. This number is the minimum buoyancy required for a normal residential dock. If you will be mooring a watercraft or think you'll be having a lot of big parties with lots of people on the dock, use 30 as the multiplier.

Every dock float has a buoyancy rating expressed in pounds per square foot (psf). The 9 × 36 × 48" float on the previous pages, for example, has a buoyancy rating of 500 psf. Thus, it would take two of these to support a 40-sq.-ft. floating dock. Because floats are sold in a very wide variety of sizes, make sure that none of the floats you plan to buy are larger than the width of your dock. If you have a shallow shoreline, bear in mind that most floats require 3 ft. of water depth, so you won't be able to run the floats all the way to the shore.

HOW TO BUILD A FLOATING DOCK

1 *Cut the frame members to length from 2 × 6 or 2 × 8 stock, as specified in your plan. Here, red cedar is being cut for the stringers and headers.*

2 *Lay out the stringer locations on the headers and then, on a flat surface, tack the frame members together with deck screws. Use a small square to check the corners as you work, but use a more reliable method (such as measuring the diagonals) once the frame is together.*

FLOATING THAT LOAD

Now that you've figured out how much to float, you'll need to figure out what to float it with.

First off, let's look at some things **not** to float your dock with. These may be cheap options and there may be promises made. You may have seen them on docks where they looked okay, but do yourself a favor and trust me, you don't want to use the following.

Unsuitable floatation devices

Open-Cell EPS. EPS stands for Expanded Poly-Styrene. Sure enough, this will float things, for a while. But come back in a couple of years or so and see what you think then. Open-cell EPS, you would notice, is extremely fragile—you can usually crush it into dust between your fingers. Open-cell EPS isn't designed to be used for dock floatation.

Drums. You'll encounter the term drum below in a more positive context, so let's dismiss the other kind and never mention it again here. When you think of a 55-gallon drum, this is what you think of. Now, think of all the decorations you picture when you think of such drums—

death's-heads, flammable symbols, biohazard symbols, and so on. Even where these drums are professed by their sellers to be clean, don't chance it. Like open-cell EPS, the use of reused drums (both plastic and metal) is banned on most waterfronts.

Suitable Floatation Devices

Almost every sort of floatation device you will consider will involve affixing the floats to the decking and frame. We will consider these first, and later will have a quick look at some options that will require additional construction.

Dedicated float drums are the floatation devices you are most likely to encounter. At their simplest, they are just an air-filled drum (actually more of a box, or if you've ever looked in the alleys and courtyards of large apartment or office buildings, oversized rat traps). The shell is made usually from HDPE plastic, but sometimes they are made of fiberglass. Like drums above do in theory, the shell keeps water out, and holds up the dock. Unlike the drums described above, these are specifically manufactured with the intention of holding your dock up.

3 *Add screws at each joint once the frame is squared and then attach crossers to the underside of the frame to stiffen it. A pair of evenly spaced crossers should be adequate.*

4 *Select the dock corner hardware that's best for your dock and position it as directed. Clamp it to the frame to hold it in position while you mark drilling locations. Remove the hardware.*

5 *Reinforce the joints between crossers and the stringers with hot-dipped galvanized or stainless-steel corner brackets attached with carriage bolts. To keep the bolts from tearing into the soft cedar, install a predrilled metal mounting plate on the bottom of the crosser, aligned with the holes in the corner bracket. Keep crossers well clear of any drilling points laid out in the previous step. Note: crossers should be positioned so they do not fall in float locations.*

6 *Drill guide holes for carriage bolts and install the corner hardware. Install all four corners loosely, check to make sure the frame is still square, and then tighten the bolts at each corner.*

Though hollow float drums will work, and will keep your dock afloat, the fact that they are hollow creates one significant potential problem: puncture. As with a hole in anything, a hole in a float will cause the float to begin to take on water, resulting in a less stable or sagging dock. Because they are built specifically for installation on docks, this isn't the end of the world, and replacing one isn't a terribly difficult task.

Most float drums have lips through which they are attached with screws or bolts to the dock frame, so if damage occurs, you simply reverse the installation process, and redo it with a new float. Additionally, because hollow float drums are empty inside, they weigh less than floats that contain filler.

Floats that are filled usually contain closed-cell or open-cell EPS foam (closed cell is preferable). When filled with foam, the drum strength is increased, better protecting it against punctures as well as ice. In the first case, the foam provides additional support to the shell—if you ever filled a whiffle bat with water and took a swing, you've noticed that you hit the ball farther, and are more likely to dent the ball than your bat—it's the same principle in filling floats with foam. Additionally, the foam goes some ways toward preventing ice from forming on the float.

Closed-cell EPS maintains its buoyancy if punctured. Open-cell EPS is generally permitted by most authorities for use as a float filler. It is cheaper to manufacture than is its closed-cell relation, and thus most manufacturers will use it instead of closed-cell EPS. The drawback to open-cell EPS is the same as when used in stand-alone applications: it takes on water much more readily than closed-cell EPS. When sealed away in their drums, the two grades of EPS provide about equal buoyancy, but buy closed-cell floats if you can find them.

A second quality measure to look for when purchasing dedicated float drums is the manufacturing process: blown or rotational. Blown molding tends to be thinner and thus less capable of withstanding puncture than plastic formed with rotational molding. Find out which process was used, because you may not notice a difference in price.

7 Continue attaching connector hardware and hinges as indicated in your dock plan. If you are building multiple sections, lay the sections next to one another while laying out locations for hinges and connectors.

8 If your floating dock will be anchored with pipes, attach sleeves at the outer edges of the dock and as indicated in your dock kit manufacturer's instructions. If you will be anchoring the docks with weights and cables, see page 107.

9 *Cut the deck boards to length by setting up a stop on the table of your power miter saw. Alternately, cut the deck boards slightly too long so you can come back and trim them to length with a single guided cut once they're all installed.*

10 *Begin installing the deck boards, using a pair of 2½" deck screws at each joint. There are several strategies for doing the deck-board installation, including the one shown here: start in the very middle and work out symmetrically toward each end.*

Although the air-or foam-filled square plastic drum comprise virtually all of the residential float market, you will find a few oddball products out there. One variant is a plastic drum filled with 80 plastic 2-liter-type bottles. Manufactured by Coast Marine of Canada (see Resources, page 124), these *enviro-floats* offer the basic floatation of a hollow drum with the secondary floatation of each of these air-filled vessels. Thus, if the shell and one or several of the vessels are ruptured, there are a lot of helpers to prevent your dock from sagging. The 50" × 27½" models boast a load capacity of 625 pounds each.

Another option you may encounter is recycled tires filled with foam. The original version of this was known as the *Topper Float.* To make these floats, open-cell EPS was enclosed in recycled tires, sealed up with plywood on either side, and bolted to the bottom of the dock frame. Though claiming a life expectancy of 20 years, users began noticing that after about 5 years, floats would lose their buoyancy and begin to sag. At the same time, this was a very popular design—inexpensive and easy to install.

A company now called Jibb's Dock Floats began manufacturing its own version of the Topper float using a closed-cell EPS manufactured by Dow. These, unlike their open-cell predecessors, tended not to degrade to the same degree, and because they were closed cell, did not take on water to such a degree that it became such an immediate issue for floatation.

They are convenient as floats, requiring only that you predrill holes for the bolts, and have the benefit of being easily and individually replaced when they begin to lose buoyancy.

A relative newcomer in the past decade to dock floatation is *HDPE pipe* that is sometimes filled with foam, and factory sealed or capped to create a water-impermeable floatation device that is then bolted to your frame. These are quite durable, boasting of a resistance to abrasion and puncture that compares well with steel pipes. Looking a bit like pontoons, they come in various sizes. As a rule, these floats come in pairs with clamps fitted with tabs that allow you to quite easily bolt them to your frame.

11 *Fill in the remaining deck boards, ripping the final board to width if necessary.*

12 *With a helper, flip the dock section over onto the decking side to gain access for installing the floats.*

13 *Set the floats into (or onto, depending on your plan) the underside of the dock. If you have followed your plan correctly, the floats should fit neatly between any crossers that are attached to the bottom of the dock framing.*

14 *Attach the floats to the frame using the hardware specified by the float manufacturer.*

If you'd rather not go through the labor of building a dock frame, there are a number of alternatives that are essentially floatation devices doing double duty as framing. By using these dedicated floats as a frame as well, you lower the center of gravity of your structure, and thus increase its stability.

One product that doubles as float and frame is *HDPE pipe.* While HDPE pipe comes in a float-only form that will allow you to bolt the frame you built onto the floats, you can also find products, such as the Waverider, to which decking can be applied directly.

Float drum frames are quite similar to common float drums, but are built in such a way that they take up part of your framing. Thus, instead of outside stringers, the floats themselves provide structural support for the whole dock—you affix headers to the floats themselves, and a support beam in the middle, and voila!—just affix your decking and you're good to go.

Steel pipes are stronger than wood, and, whether hollow or foam filled, will provide you with a durability and strength unparalleled by any other floatation material. The only problem with steel is that if you should use hollow steel tubing, if rust or anything else should cause the tube to be punctured, the whole thing (decking included) will sink like a rock. Steel tubes are usually fitted, like HDPE pipes, to allow you to easily attach supports and decking. Docks that utilize steel tubes are terribly heavy on land, but once in water, are a very durable and solid alternative to other forms of floatation. Moreover, you can expect them to last at least 20 years (often, and if properly coated, much longer), so the initial cost outlay is offset by a worry-free structure and floatation device for many years.

15 *Apply finish if desired (a semitransparent deck stain is a good choice) and then attach accessories, such as dock bumpers.*

Foam Billets. If you enjoy working with wood, you might consider building a dock that relies on extruded foam billets made of closed-cell EPS. Because EPS tends to be a great deal more fragile than steel or PE, open-cell EPS must be doubly encapsulated to prevent breakup.

When using closed-cell EPS, you'll want to choose billets that are not molded, which means that they will be referred to as extruded EPS, and this means that it is formed under pressure, creating a billet in which the molecules are all going in one direction, creating a stronger substance. Simple molding, by contrast, just involves pouring the molten polystyrene into a mold, and so the molecules go in all different directions, actually working against the strength of the whole structure.

Closed-cell EPS billets need to be wrapped in a protective mesh, often referred to as sand screen—primarily because it is similar to drywall sand screens. Because the holes in sandscreen are so small, animals (who will also have access to your dock) can't get through to the polystyrene that would provide nice insulation for a nest. Unless you want to give squirrels, raccoons, and other critters such a thoughtful housewarming present, avoid the traditional chicken-wire wrap, which offers plenty of access for a squirrel to gain entry.

Not only do foam billets need to be encased in a protective mesh, they also need to be protected with a subframe. A subframe protects your billets and provides extra weight to your structure to keep the whole thing from being top-heavy. The subframe is built around the billets and affixed to your frame, or you would simply build a double decker with the foam billets encased in the lower deck.

Some aluminum docks include aluminum decking, while others (such as the one above) have aluminum primarily in structural locations. Custom docks purchased made-to-order, such as the Shoremaster model shown here, typically have light but strong aluminum frames and leg systems.

ALUMINUM DOCKS

Aluminum docks make up a fairly broad category, with the majority falling into the roll-in or made-to-order category. Often featuring support rails of trusslike aluminum webs, these docks are lightweight and made for easy installation and removal.

Another type of aluminum dock, available at many building centers, is created more for the do-it-yourselfer. Often called flip-in docks, they are assembled a bit like Tinker Toys on shore and then snapped together as each section is flipped into the water. Many, such as the one being assembled on the next page, have corrugated aluminum decking panels that require virtually no maintenance. To see this type of deck being installed, go to page 108.

HOW TO ASSEMBLE AN ALUMINUM FLIP-IN DOCK

1 *The specific assembly instructions vary from model to model, but in most cases you'll want to do as much of the flip-in dock assembly on shore as you can. Typically, you start by attaching the legs to the dock frame and support struts with bolts and nuts with lock washers. This can require getting your fingers into some tight areas, so be patient. A correctly sized closed-end wrench is very useful here.*

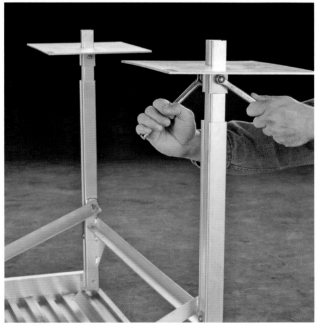

2 *Attach the adjustable footpads that fit over the legs. Don't overtighten them, as you'll likely need to adjust them once you're at the installation area.*

3 *Attach the interlocking strip (or other connector as provided) to the dock section. You may need to drill guide holes for the bolts that secure this strip.*

"Perhaps the truth depends on a walk around the lake."
~Wallace Stevens

Getting the dock into the water is a rite of spring for many people who live on a lake or river. Once you've figured out the system, you'll find that the task feels easier every year.

INSTALLING & ANCHORING DOCKS

W ELL, THUS FAR OUR DOCKS HAVE BEEN FAIRLY EASY TO BUILD, NICE TO LOOK AT, AND A WHOLE LOT OF FUN FOR THE HYPOTHETICAL FAMILIES WHO THEORETICALLY USE THEM. THE PROBLEM THAT THEY (AND YOU) WILL SOON ENCOUNTER IS GETTING THEM INTO THE WATER WHERE THEY BELONG.

There are a handful of methods you can use to create access to your new dock and to keep it securely in place. Choose the one that's right for you based on the nature of the shoreline, the size and type of dock, and the size and type of the body of water the dock will be anchored in.

In the right conditions, a dock section can be secured directly to the shoreline with just a simple mounting board. This is most often the case if you have a pipe dock being installed on a shallow, sandy shoreline, like the dock being installed in the photo above. But in many cases, you'll need a ramp or a

gangway a ramp to get from shore to dock. Fortunately, building a ramp doesn't involve a great deal more complexity than what you've just learned, and perhaps even less.

Let's say that you've built a floating dock. In most shorelines you'll find a strip of fairly shallow water followed by a steep dropoff where the floating dock is placed (most floating docks require a minimum water depth of 3 ft.). In such cases, you can build a ramp or gangway that is anchored on shore and extends out into the water until you've reached minimum depth. A ramp, at least in part,

Anchor weights are used to hold floating docks in place, or as storm anchors for any type of permanent or removable dock.

Flip-in docks allow you to install and remove your dock without ever setting foot in the water. Most have a light-weight aluminum undercarriage.

Pipes for pipe docks can be driven directly into the shore and bed.

A utility vehicle can be highly useful for getting roll-in docks in and out of the water.

is something of a dock built on land that's connected with hinges to a dock built on water. The hinges (and there are many styles) allow the dock section to move up and down as the water level changes, but without breaking or weakening the connection to the ramp.

Ramps and gangways are not the only anchoring options for docks that require a transition from the shore. One other way is to construct a ramp using a mounting board or a landing platform. A mounting board is really just what it sounds like: a simple board with a support system sunk into the ground to which one end of the ramp is attached. This is perhaps a bit clumsier means of attaching your dock to land, but it works a lot better than simply flopping the ramp onto shore. And because it requires only a couple of boards, you'll likely find yourself hopping over and onto the ramp, but it's an inexpensive method that requires only your ability to join two boards together, then sink a few screws for the hinge, and, finally, drive the assembly into the ground.

A bit more complex than a mounting board, a landing platform provides some standing and striding room before you begin the descent onto your ramp or dock. This is a little mini land dock sunk into the land. It looks a bit nicer when combined with your ramp and dock, because, like them it has a deck. Though they don't have to be, landing platforms are usually square, and at least as wide as

your ramp. To build one, use the same system of headers, stringers, corner brackets, and decking used to build a dock section.

Both platforms and mounting boards provide a stable anchor for your ramp. The tricky part comes in affixing them to land. If the shore at your waterfront is soft, be it mud, sand, or loose gravel, then affixing your mounting board or launching platform can be accomplished simply by pounding the poles into the ground and attaching them to your anchor board or platform with sleeve brackets. Alternately, you may want to use poles that act like ice-fishing augers—these twist into the ground and can be

Install crossbracing between the legs of a pipe dock to help stabilize it. This may be done during construction or installation.

A hinged gangway can be extended to transition from a permanent deck on shore to your dock.

Steps (removable or permanent) may be necessary to access your dock from a steep shoreline.

Storm anchors, like these tire anchors, offer a last line of defense to secure docks in rough weather.

quite easily removed by the same method, allowing you to move the whole structure if you have a receding or advancing waterline.

If, on the other hand, you have a rocky shoreline, you will probably need a jackhammer to get deep enough into the rock to sink your supports. For softer rock, you will need to drill deeper than you will for hard rock—usually about 1 ft. is a good depth for harder rock, whereas 3 ft. is better for particularly soft rock.

Because drilling and jackhammering into solid rock is, shall we say, an indelicate art, the holes drilled won't take your supports snugly, so you'll need to use some method of securing your supports in the rock. One common method is to use anchoring cements. There are a number on the market that will bond metal to stone, some of which utilize environmentally friendly technologies that have been in use for centuries, and work as well as polymer-based adhesives (though at a cost). Generally speaking, the containers will carry warnings such as "Avoid skin contact," "Wear gloves," and so forth. I would recommend that you heed these warnings. Figure that if something is capable of bonding

CUSTOM DOCKS

If you're not interested in building and assembling your own dock from scratch, you can purchase a custom dock to fit your property. Many such docks employ pipes and footpads for support (above) and are put in and taken out of the water in sections. Some, such as the roll-in dock below, are fabricated on a single metal truss.

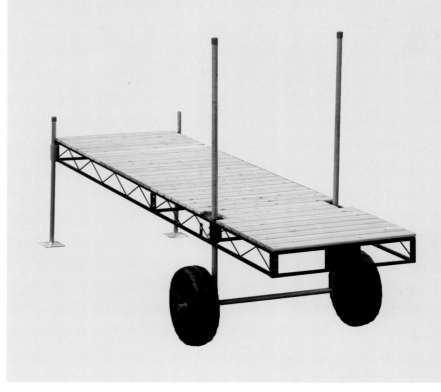

two largely non-porous things like stone and metal for all weather, it won't have much difficulty doing the same to your fingers or other appendages.

Another option for setting your pins and poles in rocky shorelines is to use rock bolts. These fit more snugly into the hole you have drilled, and are then either tapped or screwed to expand their anchors into the rock. These look something like instruments of medieval torture, but provide a very solid anchor for a launching platform or mounting board. Rock bolts are excellent for hard-rock applications, but with softer rock they tend to lose their effectiveness, likely necessitating the use of an anchoring cement.

When the above options don't work for one reason or another, there is always cement to do the trick. In the same manner by which you'd install fence posts, anchor a deck pole by digging a hole, placing your pole or pin, and pouring away.

In the event that your waterline tends to recede or advance over the season enough that you need to move your dock, you would do well to set up a series of anchor points to accommodate this over the course of the season. Thus, for example, if the waterline recedes beyond the 3 ft. of clearance necessary to keep a floating dock afloat, you may want to install an additional set of poles or pins that will allow you to move the entire assembly (ramp and dock) farther out into the water as the level drops, and to provide the necessary clearance for your dock.

HOW TO INSTALL A PIPE DOCK WITH MOUNTING BOARDS

1 Gang two or three pieces of exterior-rated lumber together and attach sleeve-and-hinge hardware to each end of the assembly.

2 Position the mounting boards near the shore and drive galvanized pipes through the sleeves. Protect the top of each pipe with a piece of scrap wood so you don't damage it when striking it with a sledge hammer or maul.

The general rule for the angle of your approach in connecting a ramp is that the absolute maximum angle you should use is 30º. That may seem pretty gradual for a staircase, but over a short distance like a dock ramp, it can feel very steep. The more gradual the angle you are able to make, the more comfortable (and safe) your descent will be. A shallower angle will require a longer ramp, of course, and as the angle approaches 30º, you will probably want to include railings.

As a rule, about 4 ft. is the minimum width for a dock ramp. As your angle approaches the 30º maximum, you'll want a still wider ramp.

If you do have a receding shoreline, and are unwilling or unable to install additional anchor points, then you might consider a rolling ramp. If you have a floating dock where the water recedes, not only is the falling waterline reducing your clearance, the traditional hinge system will also draw your dock closer into shore, further reducing the clearance the dock needs.

A rolling ramp is not difficult to build for such applications. The hardware you use resembles a rolling pin. This is then set on

3 Attach the mating-hinge hardware to the first dock section or the ramp and connect it to the hinge hardware on the mounting board.

4 Drive pipes to secure the dock sections through the attached pipe sleeves. Try to keep the sections fairly level as you work.

5 Once all the sections are installed, level the sections carefully and then tighten the set bolts securely. You can adjust the height of the dock as the water level changes by loosening and retightening the bolts.

The anchor point for your dock will involve a hinge at the anchor point. In the event that you do not experience a significant drop or advance in the water level, then another set of hinges will be quite sufficient at the dock end.

Drive a pipe through the sleeve at the shore end of a floating dock to keep it stationary. Floating-dock sleeves are not held to pipes with set bolts, so the pipe can move up and down in the sleeve as the water level changes.

a landing pad (remember, though your decking looks nice, it makes a small-circumference wheel have a harder time moving smoothly), which allows your ramp to roll in and out, depending on the water level. For this application, the ideal is to build your ramp at the high-water point, and have your ramp as close to level with the dock as possible.

The drawback to a rolling ramp, especially if your ramp is narrower than the width of your dock, is that at high water, it can significantly reduce your workable dock space.

A nonskid surface is important for dock safety, and this applies doubly to ramps and gangways,

particularly if your incline is steep. To improve traction you can install rough-surfaced grip tape to the decking. This is not the best solution, because at installation, it is uncomfortable under barefeet (it is sandpaper, after all!), and over time, as the grip becomes worn, or degrades in the sun and water, grip tape can be nearly as slippery as plain wood when wet.

A more common solution, particularly with steeper inclines, is to screw 1 × 2" slats into each plank in your ramp. These won't technically improve your traction, but they will arrest backsliding.

ANCHORING YOUR DOCK

The difference between a floating dock and a raft is that the former is held in place somewhat permanently, and in the second case, well, it isn't. Not anchoring your dock might lead to some exciting adventures, but will make your dock a great deal less convenient to access from your shorefront most of the time. Thus, most will want to forego the roaming lifestyle in favor of something a little more settled and predictable. Additionally, those who opt for a pipe dock might consider anchoring it to provide greater stability.

Anchors are simple things—pretty much anything that sinks can serve as an anchor. But not everything that sinks makes a good anchor. For example, machinery and anything with toxic or potentially toxic crud on it should be discounted.

The most common and easily made type of anchor is just an old tire with concrete poured in and a hook or other anchoring point set in the concrete. You can usually get hold of used tires for free (who knows, you may even have a few of your own), and all you need is to mix and pour the concrete, then set your anchor into it.

Homemade tire anchors are very convenient because the tire can be rolled out to launch it where you need it, and then just plopped into the water. Most docks will require several tire anchors.

Whether it's homemade or purchased, anchors are secured with cables or chains. You simply affix a cable or chain through the anchor point and drop the anchor into the water. Once dropped in the water, you'll probably want to leave the anchors where they lie and detach the cables or chains from

ROLL-IN DOCKS

If your waterfront property features a relatively smooth, shallow bed near the shore, consider purchasing a roll-in dock system. The ultimate in convenience if you need to remove the dock for the winter, many roll-in docks are custom-built to fit your property by dock equipment retailers. Or, you can buy dock wheels from dock equipment manufacturers so you can add roll-in capabilities to your homemade dock system. Roll-in docks may be used with other dock support systems, such as pipe dock hardware, or they may rely on the wheels themselves to support the dock while it's in the water (you'll still need to anchor the dock, however).

the anchor when you remove your dock (if you'd rather not dive down and reattach the cable, secure the free cable end to a float for the winter).

For a floating dock, anchors should weigh at least three times as much as the dock itself. You'll want to anchor it at the corners, usually with two anchors per corner. For this, remember your basic rectangular structure, even if you've installed decking over the top. Thus, an L-shaped dock will have not six, but eight anchors if you are anchoring the shore end as well.

Because you don't want to end up with chains and cables out in the water for swimmers and boats to run into, anchor your dock using a technique known as cross-cabling, or cross-chaining. The optimal stability would be for your anchors to be set farther out from the structure itself: You can achieve the same stability by just inverting the direction of the chains, so you get the same lateral anchoring, keeping the whole thing tucked neatly under your dock.

STORM ANCHORS

Where dock anchors should be taut to prevent your dock from sliding out from underfoot, if your waterfront is the sort of place that encounters large wakes, waves, or heavy storms, it is probable that you will want to incorporate a storm anchor into your anchoring system.

A storm anchor, unlike an ordinary anchoring system, works with a long, heavy (at least $5/8$" and sometimes weighing over 200 pounds), slack chain affixed to an anchor. The anchor is usually set well

HOW TO MAKE A DOCK ANCHOR

1 Simply lay the tire so that the hole is facing upward—a plastic sheet underneath is ideal, but you can rest it on a piece of plywood. Mix the concrete, and pour it into the hole.

2 Before the concrete sets, insert a U-bolt, making sure that at least 1" of clear opening remains between the U-bolt and the concrete. To strengthen it, add cross supports by bolting them to the threaded ends of the U-bolt. Let the whole thing dry, and you have yourself an anchor.

HOW TO INSTALL A DOCK ANCHOR

1 *When launching your tire anchors, roll them to their respective corners on the dock (generally, you should have an anchor for each corner of a floating dock like the one above).*

2 *Attach one end of the anchor chain or cable to the U-bolt set into the center of the tire anchor.*

3 *Attach the other end of the chain or cable to the corner dock hardware or an eye hook. The chain or cable should be sightly longer than the water depth at each corner.*

4 *With a helper and great care, lower the anchor into the water. For chains, move the anchor as needed until the chain is taut. For cables, tighten a turnbuckle until the cable is taut.*

out into the water, and the chain droops pretty much straight down to the lake or river bed, becoming buried in soft mud or tangled in underwater vegetation to give the whole structure greater gripping power. Thus, when harsh waves and winds hit the dock, its tendency to twist is greatly reduced by this dead weight affixed to one of its corners. Aside from acting as a backup by keeping the dock from twisting, the storm anchor limits the possibility of your cables being placed under the significant and sudden strain that could cause them to snap. To limit this possibility further, it is recommended that you place the storm anchor in such a way that the anchor end leads into the prevailing winds.

In the case of floating docks, storm anchors provide a guide that prevents the dock from drifting in, out, or side-to-side. The frame of the floating dock is fitted with a spud bracket, which is simply a sleeve that fits around the spud and prevents the dock from drifting away. The sleeve is self-adjusting to accommodate the dock's tendency to float to wherever the water level happens to be.

HOW TO INSTALL A FLIP-IN DOCK

1 Gang two or three exterior-rated boards together and attach a pair of pipe sleeves to the back face (if you already have a landing platform skip this step).

2 Drive pipes through the pipe sleeves to secure the mounting board at the edge of the water.

3 Attach a mounting strip (purchased separately from the flip-in dock manufacturer) to the mounting board.

4 *Lower the mating end of the first dock section (see page 95 for information on assembling flip-in docks) so it snaps into the mounting strip.*

5 *Adjust the dock feet so the dock section is level. Measure the water depth where the next section will end and set the feet for that section to match.*

6 *Tie a rope to the end of the next section and snap the mating strips at the section ends together.*

7 *Lower the next section into the water with the rope. If the height is not correct, raise the section back up and adjust the legs. Add remaining sections.*

"*A few days ago I walked along the edge of the lake and was treated to the crunch and rustle of leaves with each step I made. The acoustics of this season are different and all sounds, no matter how hushed, are as crisp as autumn air.*"
~ Eric Sloane

Dock accessories can do more than simply add bells and whistles to your structure; they can increase functionality, efficiency, and safety. The dock lights seen here accomplish all three goals (and add beauty, too).

A swiveling captain's chair offers an unmatched view when installed at a forward corner of your dock.

ACCESSORIZING & CUSTOMIZING YOUR DOCK

OSCAR WILDE ONCE REMARKED THAT "THE ONLY WAY TO ATONE FOR BEING A LITTLE OVER-DRESSED IS TO BE ABSOLUTELY OVER EDUCATED." WELL, AT THE MOMENT, YOUR DOCK IS OVEREDUCATED AND ABSOLUTELY UNDERDRESSED.

By now, you should have a good sense of both the physics and chemistry involved in your waterfront intrusion, and with that knowledge in mind, you can begin to accessorize your dock. It may well be that you like the broad, uninterrupted space of your dock as it is—most do. Still, many will incorporate some sort of accessory into their dock, even if it is so simple as a mooring cleat.

Though boats and docks seem to go together, they are in fact something of natural enemies. Boats banging into the dock weaken joints, crack wood, and stress dock stability. Docks, unafraid to return the favor, gouge hulls, and failing that, may conspire to leave a mark on your floating palace. Nonetheless, a well-built dock, accessorized in the proper way, can help these two cantankerous water-mates get along, or at least turn their hot war into a long-simmering cold one.

Cleats and Rings. Mooring devices are generally sized-down versions of their larger ocean-going brethren, known as bitts and bollards. Cleats provide an easy method of mooring your boat—you

Dock bumpers come in many shapes and styles. These pole-style bumpers protect your boat while offering a solid point for casting off.

Nautical cleats may be bolted or screwed to your decking, but for better holding power look for a cleat with a reinforced metal mounting bracket that is attached to the underside of the deck board.

don't have to consult your Bluejacket's Manual to tie your boat to a cleat. Whether or not the cleat is safely affixed to your dock is something of another matter. You can simply screw cleats into your decking, but it is possible to accidentally pull the cleat back out. A cleat will suffice for a very lightweight craft (such as a canoe) that won't be moored there most of the time, but anything much larger won't stay moored there for too long. A better option is to back each cleat with a metal bracket. These look like shelves made of galvanized or stainless steel.

Some deck cleats are recessed for safety. When not in use, they simply flop down into their little coffins where they stay out of the way until you need them. The recess is cut into the decking with a router and the cleat apparatus is then bolted through the decking to a cleat bracket beneath.

Rings. Rings require more knot-tying know-how than cleats. In their simplest form, a bracket with a ring running through it sits proud on top of the deck. Also like cleats, these come in recessed

versions, which again require routing of your deck to get them beneath the grade of your deck.

Bumpers and Fenders. The most traditional dock bumper has been the old rubber tire. But tires don't offer good protection to your boat, and it is virtually impossible to solidly affix them so they don't work free. The only places you should have

Gear towers can be tall or short and are used to temporarily stow boating gear or tackle. They can even be used as a shoreside kitchenette or bar.

To buffer your dock and boat, use genuine dock bumpers, like this vinyl strip bumper, not makeshift solutions like old tires or empty bleach bottles.

tires on your dock are to anchor it or float it. Look for dedicated bumpers for your dock—they are worth the investment. Dock bumpers are usually long strips of vinyl that are screwed into the outside stringers of the dock. At the very least, these provide abrasion resistance, and keep dock corners away from the hull of your boat. Other types of bumpers resemble a pillow: they are made from polyester and filled with closed-cell EPS to offer a nice soft cover for your corners. Unlike traditional vinyl bumpers, they are easily removed.

Often, one will find that folks who sell dedicated dock bumpers will also sell L-shaped corner fenders. These are nice and quite convenient to install if you have the extra money—your lead corners are thus hidden behind a layer of vinyl, and they complete the vinyl skirt you have just taken time to install.

Another option for your lead corners—the place on your dock most closely resembling an ice-pick—is to install bumper wheels, sometimes called roller bumpers, designed specifically to keep your boat sufficiently far afield from your corners, and help to guide your boat into its resting place.

Ladders. Perhaps the most common of all nonboating accessories you will consider for your dock will be a ladder. Most dock ladders are metal.

Swimming ladders are important to the safe enjoyment of your dock. Some have the traditional ladder appearance, while others have a single pole, resembling a pogo stick.

Because they are exposed for all to see, you may want to splurge a bit here and go for a stainless-steel ladder instead of a galvanized steel or aluminum ladder. A properly installed ladder will have a backing plate and sturdy bolts and washers on a DIY wood-frame dock. Most kit docks include ladders designed to work with their platform.

Benches and Chairs. For most, dragging chairs to and from the dock is not a particularly pleasant way of arranging for seating. What's worse is that deck chairs are either heavy, making this task

Dock kits with high-strength undercarriages often make available "off-deck" accessories like this bench that hooks onto the undercarriage and cantilevers out over the water.

cumbersome, or have a tendency to blow over and into the water. For this reason, many choose to install some form of permanent seating, usually in the form of one or several benches and perhaps a swiveling captain's chair or two (see page 112).

Benches, unlike chairs, provide fairly versatile seating or lounging arrangements. Placed in conjunction to one another, one can easily create a very nice space for the family to gather round, particularly when a table is added. They can be affixed to docks in any number of ways. As with most of the things you've learned to build thus far, a bench works best when its weight is distributed as evenly as is possible, and where feasible, makes some use of underlying stringers.

Dock Boxes. While some will build their boxes straight into their benches, this does prove a bit of a hassle for some, as people don't always enjoy getting up from conversation because you forgot to get the fishing net. Thus, a number of dock boxes are available.

Today, a typical dock box is plastic and fitted with brackets that allow you to bolt it directly to the deck. This is just about as uncomplicated as it gets—you've got a box, you bolt it down, and you put stuff in it. The only issue with this is that you lose as much deck space as the box takes up (dock boxes often are used for seating, but they aren't generally designed for this purpose).

A combination of permanent and portable seating offers flexibility for docks that are used for entertaining and enjoyment.

A waterproof plastic box is a good option if you only plan to store dry things, but if your list of storables includes life jackets, fishing gear, and other wet items, shop for a box that allows drainage out the bottom. Or, find a plan and build your own.

Dog Ramps. While most are only too happy to let their doggies have a bit of a swim, getting them back onto dry land is often a dangerous endeavor. A company called PupGear has invented a portable (or permanent, if you wish) ramp for the dockside that allows your dog to climb back up onto the dock quite easily. These anchor either using a permanent bracket, or by making use of a standard mooring cleat that it fits over. The water end uses an adjustable float to provide in-water access for your pooch.

A homemade dock box can be customized to your needs and attached directly to the dock structure. Most have drainage capabilities in the bottom panel.

Many boat-lift systems are designed to attach to the structural system of your dock.

Personal watercraft are common enough now that PWC hoists are easy to find for them.

Hoists and Lifts. If you own a boat and don't want to store it permanently on a trailer, you'll want to invest in a boat lift. Often, a lift or a hoist is incorporated directly into the dock structure, for reasons of security as well as convenience. The most inexpensive lifts, suitable for smaller fishing boats, canoes, and other light craft, have a hand-cranked winch that raises the boat and the lift up out of the water—or at least far enough out that the boat won't float away. Heavier models designed for

Often made of structural aluminum, boat hoists are very important pieces of equipment for your waterfront activities. Not only do they protect your watercraft by lifting it out of the water, they allow you to lock up your boats while you are away.

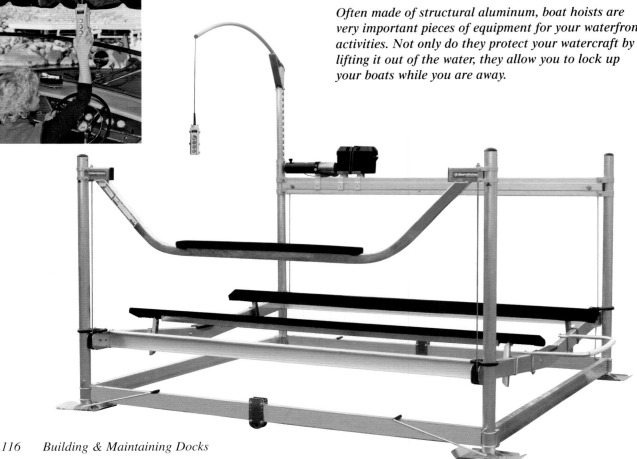

Not all accessories are attached permanently to the dock. This inflatable swimming trampoline floats, but without the dock to attach it to you'd have to use an anchor or other type of mooring to keep it from floating away.

Dock-equipment supply catalogs are filled with possibilities for your dock, such as this dock-mounted flag pole. See Resources, page 124.

larger craft have heavy-duty motors, usually electric, that drive the lift. Most boat lifts are equipped with locks and other useful security features.

Tents and Awnings. The most common tent varieties are usually incorporated into pipe docks. The tops of the dock's pipes act as anchors, and the tent poles are simply slid over the top. Because not everyone is going to have a pipe dock, this same structure can be effected quite simply by bolting feet to the deck. In the exact same fashion, tent poles are slid into the form-fitted feet or around them, and usually cinch-bolted in place, and can be easily removed. For folks who have built a slip for their boats, this is a very common application, and keeps the sun and rain off your boat when you're not out on the open water.

Gazebos. A gazebo is essentially a permanent tent, or at least that's the way I think about it. Unlike a tent or awning, though, it adds significant weight to your dock. On the plus side, it tends not to act like a giant parachute. A gazebo is not the sort of thing folks who need to remove their docks in winter will likely want to deal with. It is possible, but it is something of a major hassle.

Because a gazebo can involve doubling, even tripling the weight of your dock, depending on the elaborateness of the structure, many will want to build theirs straight into the deck, using the deck floor as the floor to their gazebo. This does work, but you will find that the resulting structure is oftentimes not quite so sturdy as if you had built the additional deck.

Swabbing the deck is just as important a chore for a landlubber with a wood dock as it is for the first mate aboard a tiny ship. Use environmentally safe detergent and wash with a power washer or do it the old-fashioned way by scrubbing with a stiff-bristled, long-handled scrub brush (inset photo).

REPAIRING & MAINTAINING DOCKS

WHETHER YOU LIKE IT OR NOT, YOU WILL UNDOUBTEDLY FIND YOURSELF HAVING TO FIX YOUR BELOVED DOCK AT SOME POINT OR OTHER. HAVING DONE CAREFUL CARPENTRY TO THIS POINT IS A BIG HELP— THE STANDARDIZATION AND CAREFUL MEASUREMENT EMPHASIZED ABOVE MAKE REPLACING PARTS EASIER, EVEN IF REPLACING PARTS IS SELDOM EASY. IN SHORT, A DOCK IN NEED OF REPAIRS AND UPKEEP IS NOT THE END OF THE WORLD. BUT YOU SHOULD MAKE EVERY EFFORT TO CORRECT PROBLEMS AS SOON AS YOU CAN.

Docks require both seasonal maintenance and occasional repairs. Regular maintenance chores include cleaning the deck and resealing if you used a deck sealer, sweeping and monitoring the gaps between deck boards for organic matter buildup, cleaning submerged posts to get rid of algae, and checking for damage from borers.

The most common repair issue with wood docks is splitting or rotting decking. This is, fortunately, tan easy repair to effect: simply remove and replace the rotten board with a new one.

If your decking is showing rot, chances are your wood framing may be degrading as well. It is possible to repair rotten framing members in the water,

Use metal cleaner and polish to treat metal dock parts, such as this stainless-steel dock ladder. Clean and polish the parts before storing for the winter.

Remove dock decking sections (if they are removable) in your dock and let them dry thoroughly before you cover them for winter storage.

but this is usually not the easiest or most pleasant way of doing the job. Whenever you can, remove the dock from the water first. This is true of all maintenance and upkeep tasks, including any that might risk introducing chemicals into the water.

If you decided to go with removable decking, then your job in replacing framing members will be that much easier. Otherwise, you're looking at replacing something that not only supports the decking, but also has some structural duty as well. No matter how well you built your dock, and even if you used the appropriate fasteners and corner brackets, the wear and tear on the dock can lead to having to replace one or several of these members.

The best way to go about this rather cumbersome task is one at a time. Because you are into the

Visually inspect dock wood from below and above for signs of rot.

nether regions of your dock, you'll need to replace each header or stringer individually. If you are discovering rot where the builder endeavored to hold the whole dock together with screws and/or nails instead of corner brackets, this is the perfect opportunity for you to right his or her errors.

Floating docks eventually will fail. If you start to notice sagging, first check to make sure the floats are positioned correctly relative to the frame. Moving floats so that they are at least in part directly under headers and stringers creates a greater likelihood that your dock will work all in concert with itself, and wobble less. But regardless of the materials they are made of, dock floats take on water. In many cases, they can be fixed (see next page).

HOW TO REPAIR A FLOAT

The gash in this PE plastic dock float looks like it could be terminal, but there are a few DIY friendly plastic repair products you can use on it. First, pry at the gash to try to get it to close up as best you can.

Heat the area around the damage with the secondary flame of a propane or MAPS torch (see photo, above) to degloss the PE plastic so the repair compound will bind.

Apply the repair compound as instructed. Here, a product called Marine-Tex Poly-Dura is being applied with a syringe.

FLOAT REPAIR

If your air-filled floats are punctured, the easiest way to repair the polyethylene plastic is to remove the drum and take it to an auto-body repair shop (no kidding!). Because most cars make use of PE in some form or other, repairing a crack in the plastic on a car is no different from repairing a crack on your float drum—they can create a professional and seamless repair (better than what you need!) that should put any worries to rest about the job done.

The trouble with that solution is, well, it involves mechanics, who tend not to be cheap. The benefit is that it's easy.

You can make the repair yourself, too, using one of a variety of similar methods. ordinary flame on a blow-torch to slightly melt the area around the crack or puncture (not completely, just to soften it), and pour molten PE into the crack, smooth the matter up with a putty knife, let it dry, and you're all set.

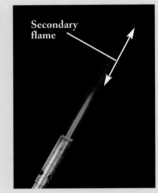

Use the cooler, light blue portion of the torch flame (called the secondary flame) to condition PE plastic.

An easier method is to use an epoxy such as Marine-Tex Poly-Dura. For this, you'll need to degloss the area around the puncture with the secondary flame from a propane or MAPS-fueled torch. Because PE is a waxy sort of plastic, this is essential to create a solid bond. Next, simply squeeze the epoxy over the crack, shore it up with a putty knife, and allow to cure for at least 24 hours. Though this product can be applied even in the water, you don't want to stress your patch, so it is a good idea to do the repair out of water, if possible.

An alternative product to the epoxy system (which is fairly expensive) is delivered with an ordinary glue gun. Polyethylene sticks (See Resources) are heated with a common glue gun, and smoothed out with a putty knife, and should be just as strong as the rest of the float shell.

HOW TO RENEW A DOCK DECK

Drive new fasteners to replace any rusted, corroded, or broken ones. Choose a fastener that's slightly longer than the one you're replacing, and fill old screwholes or nail holes with epoxy.

Working on shore in a safe work area when possible, spray the decking with a commercial deckwashing solution, using a hand sprayer. Allow the cleaner sufficient time to work (see label).

Scrub the dock deck boards thoroughly, wearing waterproof protective gloves and eye protection.

Rinse the deck thoroughly with clean water. If the deck was finished with deck stain, reapply with a long-handle roller or paint pad after the decking has dried for a few days.

HOW TO REPAIR A ROTTED WOOD DOCK

Remove old nails or screws from the damaged area, using a cat's paw or other pry bar (or a screwgun if you can get the tip into the old screwhead).

Inspect the stringers for rot and other damage by probing with an awl or a screwdriver.

If you identify dry rot or other forms of damage, it is possible to repair it if the damage is confined to a relatively small area. Start by removing the rotted wood until you have exposed sound wood. If the damage extends more than halfway through the board, replace the board.

Apply a heavy coat of sealer/preservative to the damaged area. Let it dry and then apply a second coat. Meanwhile, cut a reinforcing stringer (called a sister) that is the same width and thickness as the damaged board. The reinforcing board should extend at least 12" past each end of the damaged area.

Treat all sides of the sister stringer with wood preservative and then, once it is dry, attach it to the damaged stringer with 10d galvanized nails.

At the edges of the dock frame, attach the stringer to the mating stringer or header by toe-nailing. Predrill to avoid splitting the wood.

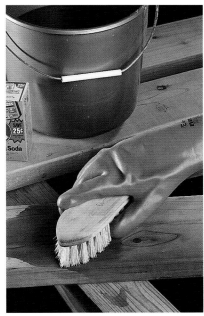

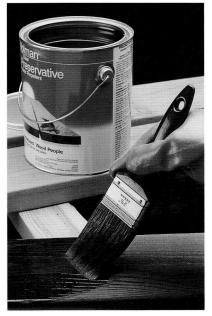

Before attaching replacement deck boards, you can age them slightly by brushing the boards with a mixture of 1 cup baking soda to 1 gallon water. This way they will blend in better with their neighboring deck boards.

Apply a coat of sealer/preservative or deck stain to all sides of the new deck boards.

Attach the new deck boards to the repaired dock frame with galvanized, coated, or stainless-steel deck screws.

RESOURCES

Black & Decker
Portable power tools
www.blackanddecker.com
800-544-6986

Great Northern Docks
Docks and dock building components
www.greatnortherndocks.com
800-423-4042
sales@greatnortherndocks.com

Marine-Tex Poly-Dura kit
Specialty plastics adhesive
(Repair polyethylene dock floats)
www.marinetex.com
215-855-8450
sales@itwprc.com

PortaDock, Inc.
Aluminum docks, lifts and accessories
www.portadock.com
218-847-5459
800-435-5459

ShoreLand'r
Boat and PWC trailers
Midwest Industries
www.midwestindustries.com
800-859-3028

ShoreStation
Docks, hoists and accessories
Midwest Industries
www.midwestindustries.com
800-859-3028

West Marine
Dock and docking supplies
(retail and Internet)
www.westmarine.com
800-685-4838

PHOTO CREDITS

Photography Contributers

Great Northern Docks
www.greatnortherndocks.com
800-423-4042
page 100 (top left).

Hewitt Roll-a-dock
www.hewitt-roll-a-dock.com
1-800-544-2067
page 39.

Palm Beach Marinecraft, Inc.
www.palmbeachmarine.com
507-233-8020
page 28 (bottom)

Porta Dock, Inc.
www.portadock.com
800-435-5459
pages 8 (bottom), 9 (bottom), 14-15, 48-49,
84 (bottom), 101 (both), 114 (top right).

ShoreStation
www.shorestation.com
800-859-3028
pages: 8 (top), 10 (both), 11 (both),
13 (top), 17, 30 (both), 32 (both), 34, 36 (top),
58 (top), 94 (top), 99 (top right, bottom right),
100 (top right, bottom left), 105, 112 (both),
113 (top left), 114 (top right, bottom), 115
(top), 116 (all), 117 (both).

Photographers

Alamy, Ltd.
©britishcolumbiaphotos.com/ Alamy: page
82; © Dennis Hallinan/ Alamy: pages 72-73.

Billy Lindner Photography
www.blpstudio.com
© Bill Lindner: pages 4-5, 110-111.

INDEX

Also from

CREATIVE PUBLISHING INTERNATIONAL

Complete Guide to Bathrooms
Complete Guide to Ceramic & Stone Tile
Complete Guide to Creative Landscapes
Complete Guide to Decks
Complete Guide to Easy Woodworking Projects
Complete Guide to Finishing Walls & Ceilings
Complete Guide to Flooring
Complete Guide to Home Carpentry
Complete Guide to Home Plumbing
Complete Guide to Home Wiring
Complete Guide to Kitchens
Complete Guide to Landscape Construction
Complete Guide to Masonry & Stonework
Complete Guide to Outdoor Wood Projects
Complete Guide to Painting & Decorating
Complete Guide to Roofing & Siding
Complete Guide to Trim & Finish Carpentry
Complete Guide to Windows & Doors
Complete Guide to Wood Storage Projects
Complete Guide to Yard & Garden Features
Complete Outdoor Builder
Complete Photo Guide to Home Repair
Complete Photo Guide to Home Improvement

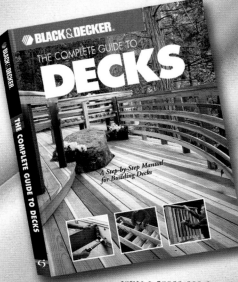

ISBN 1-58923-200-3

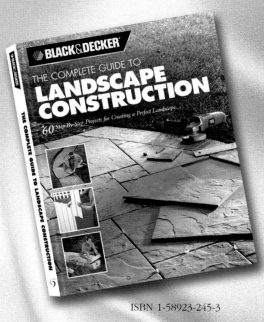

ISBN 1-58923-245-3

CREATIVE PUBLISHING INTERNATIONAL

18705 LAKE DRIVE EAST
CHANHASSEN, MN 55317

WWW.CREATIVEPUB.COM